THE
BLESSED
HOME

FROM CHAOS TO CALM
HOW YOUR WORDS CAN HEAL YOUR HOME

AMY JAE

BALBOA.PRESS
A DIVISION OF HAY HOUSE

Balboa Press books may be ordered through booksellers or by contacting:

Balboa Press
A Division of Hay House
1663 Liberty Drive
Bloomington, IN 47403
www.balboapress.com
1 (877) 407-4847

Print information available on the last page.

ISBN: 978-1-9822-4498-9 (sc)
ISBN: 978-1-9822-4499-6 (e)

Balboa Press rev. date: 08/21/2020

For Katie,
whose question sparked
this journey

Your courage and determination to create a wonderful childhood for your boys moves me deeply. Our story has been a large part of my own healing journey and I am forever grateful that God gave me such a beautiful, strong and caring daughter!

May your home be filled with laughter, compassion, wisdom and love.

Visit www.amyjae.com today to:

- Receive Amy's free emails with practical Blessing tips
- Download your free Home Blessing Planner as well as audio Morning and Evening blessings
- Find additional resources to help you create a life that you don't need to escape
- Stay updated on upcoming events, giveaways, retreats and webinars
- Purchase additional copies of *The Blessed Home* for friends and family members
- Learn how you can invite Amy Jae to speak to your group or organization

Contents

Part 4 — Blessing Guide

Resources

A Note to the Reader

This book wanted to be written … in fact, it insisted!

On a cold February afternoon, I stopped mid-sentence in writing another book to take a phone call from my daughter in California. With an active toddler and her second baby due in four weeks, she found herself facing the stress of an unexpected move. I listened as she described apartment options and rattled off a long list of things she needed to accomplish before her due date.

Suddenly, she changed direction and asked a seemingly random question: "Do you know how to do a home blessing?"

Sure … I'll send you something. I promised without hesitation, surprised and happy that she had asked.

After our phone call ended, I decided to jot down a few ideas before returning to my writing project. It wouldn't take more than 15 minutes. After all, homes are my "thing." My husband and I had renovated several homes so I knew how to design lovely spaces. On the spiritual side of things, I had attended several home blessings conducted through our church. For over a decade, we had welcomed guests from around the world to the peaceful woodland sanctuary of our bed and breakfast.

Sending a few home blessing ideas in an email would be easy.

An hour later, I knew I was in trouble. It turns out that I couldn't just "jot down a few ideas." Each sentence I wrote unleashed a flood of memories and more ideas. The sentences grew into paragraphs, chapters and sections. The hour became days, weeks, months and ultimately a writing journey of three years.

As the memories, emotions and thoughts tumbled out of me, I heard an ancient, almost forgotten practice knocking on the door of our modern lives. In a world facing epidemic levels of stress, depression, anxiety and hatred, Blessing kindly asked to be re-invited into the most sacred of all places - our homes.

In these pages, you will not find tips for making your home pretty. You have Pinterest and HGTV for that! Nor will you find in-depth research, case studies or footnotes. I learn most of my life lessons by living right in the middle of the messy questions until I am ready to hear the answers. Answers that come to me in so many ways that I could never catalog all of their sources. Filled with stories and examples from over 20 years of "living-the-questions" learning, The Blessed Home book tells the story of my search to find a place where I belong – a home not just for my body, but most importantly, for my heart and soul.

My life story began in a devoutly Christian home so you will see traces of that influence throughout these pages. However, you do not need to embrace a Christian belief system in order to create a Blessed Home. People from all religions and cultures have practiced Blessing for generations. I trust you, dear reader, to apply these ideas to your own life story in ways that are meaningful for you. My desire is to re-introduce this beautiful and powerful lifestyle to our modern world.

The book you hold in your hands is an invitation. If you listen, you will hear Blessing knocking, urging you to open your heart and embrace a new understanding of home. In quiet moments when the ache stirs deep within, Blessing invites you to see weariness, depression, loneliness, illness, financial stress and all other struggles as portals through which healing and joy can enter your home. And finally, Blessing desires to flow through the power of your words, enabling you to create a true sanctuary where you and your family can flourish.

In The Blessed Home, we will explore:

- how your daily choices (and the choices of those who lived in your home before you) affect your home
- simple methods to cleanse and reset the atmosphere of your home.

- listening to the messages your home is sending
- filling your home with the qualities your heart truly desires.
- tools to bless your home and create a fresh start whenever you need one. Multiple times a day if you want!
- a special Home Blessing Ceremony for a new home or beginning a new chapter of life in your current home.

The home you've always imagined is not a fantasy reserved for a lucky few. The doorway to a peaceful, loving home swings open through the beautiful gift of Blessing.

Do you hear the knocking? Let's open the door and begin ...

May your past be a
pleasant memory,

Your future filled with
delight and mystery,

Your now a glorious
moment,
That fills your life with
deep contentment.

IRISH BLESSING

PART 1

Home

Where It All Begins

Close your eyes for a moment and imagine your childhood home. Take a few breaths and let yourself return to wherever that home is for you. What memories or sensations arise?

You may recall the smell of baking cookies. The sound of sheets flapping in the breeze. The streetlight illuminating your bedroom at night. The wail of sirens. The slam of car doors. The murmur of voices downstairs. The squeak of your sister practicing her violin. The splash of hot water as you shower. The joy of your dog licking your face. The taste of your grandma's lasagna. The sounds of your bicycle tires on the pavement.

Or perhaps you remember feeling lonely in the dark. The shouts of angry voices from the next room. The smell of beer on your parent's breath. The cramping of your hungry stomach. The cold when the electricity was shut off. The shame of wearing out-dated clothes from the thrift shop. The endless cycle of babysitters. The quiet of the empty house when you came home from school. The bullying of your older sibling. The slap across your face when you made a mistake. The feeling of never being good enough. The deep pain when your parents divorced.

You may have vivid memories of sight, sound and smell. Or you may experience a more general sensation – a hard-to-describe-but-familiar feeling that seems ingrained at your cellular level. Thoughts of home may inspire warmth and nostalgia. Or this whole topic may trigger you in ways that feel uncomfortable, irritating or even repulsive.

Over 7.5 billion people call planet earth home and if we each did this exercise, we would describe over 7.5 billion different memories. Even siblings growing up in the same home with the same parents tell very different versions of their childhoods. We all experience home in a uniquely personal way.

No matter what just came to your mind, I would be willing to bet that your first thought was not the memory of how perfectly the couch pillows matched the rug. Instinctively, we know that home has little to do with the actual structure we dwell in or the belongings that surround us. Around the world, we can find happy people living in huts and miserable people living in mansions.

So what makes a home?

The Oxford English Dictionary defines home as "a place where a thing flourishes or from which it originates." If you were a flower, home would be the soil into which you were planted. The place where you send down roots seeking the nourishment needed to grow. Some of us receive that nourishment and thrive in an environment of warmth, love, security and fun. Others shrivel at the memory of hunger, loneliness, abuse and fear.

Simply put, home is where you are made.

Day in and day out, through a thousand routines and rituals so ordinary that you don't even remember most of them, you become you. Your personality develops. Your social skills take shape. Your worldview forms. Your home is growing a human.

Years pass. You grow up, move out and before you know it, you have the responsibility for a house, a job, a dog and possibly a few little humans of your own.

When you think about it, creating a home may be the single most important thing we do in our lifetime and yet, we receive almost no training on how to do it well.

Getting Home Right

I chuckle every time I see a high school student carrying a plastic doll for their Home EC class. A baby that can be fed and silenced with the push of a button hardly prepares one to be a parent, yet most of us are sent out into the world armed with a few high school lessons on budgeting, birth control and baking cupcakes! If we're lucky, we have good role models to follow. In some cases, our childhood home serves more as an example of how NOT to create a home. Either way, a lot is left to chance.

Despite this meager training, our instincts tell us that home is important and we work hard to get it right. Home good sales run in the billions annually and home improvement shows boast some of the highest ratings on TV. We spend hours scouring Pinterest boards and design blogs in search of decorating inspiration and tips for organizing our homes. Perhaps if we can just get the right combination of colors, fabrics, furniture … maybe that new grill or hot tub … we will have succeeded in creating a home that we can feel good about.

And yet we don't feel good. Each new purchase or burst of creative energy brings a few moments of joy, but we soon return to feeling exhausted, stressed and empty inside. No matter how many weekend projects we complete, how many vacations we take or how many happy family pictures we post on social media, the truth hovers just beneath the surface: Making a home is VERY HARD WORK and most of us feel like we're failing at it.

I know I did.

My friends knew me as a busy, happy mom who juggled a growing family, a part-time job, house renovations, volunteer commitments and still found time to bake my own bread. Underneath all of this activity lay a very different reality. Countless nights, I stared at the ceiling wondering what I was doing wrong. Outwardly, I had created the home and family I'd always wanted. I should have been happy and grateful. But in the quiet of my own heart, I faced the stark truth.

My life looked and felt nothing like the life I'd imagined.

I knew how to select the perfect shower curtain, plant a stunning bed of perennials and make yogurt in a picnic cooler, but I had no idea how to create a real home. I felt completely inadequate for the needs of my children and the painful struggle within myself.

Millions of us have awkward relationships with home - and for some good reasons. Those who've lived with abusive or addicted parents have experienced intense fear or pain in the place that was supposed to protect them. Mental illness causes many children to assume the role of caregiver for the very person who should care for them. Foster children pay the price for their parents' struggles as they are uprooted from the only homes they've known and dropped on the doorsteps of strangers – often enduring multiple placements. Job transfers or medical crisis can send a family across the country to begin all over again in new schools and neighborhoods. Military children may adapt to the cycle of constant moves, but later in life, many feel like they don't have roots or a home town. Even in stable homes, one child's experience can be very different from another based on personality and their ability to connect at a meaningful level with their parents.

All of these situations and more can shatter (or at least shake) one's sense of safety and belonging. When it is time to create our own homes, deep emotions are triggered. We may not consciously realize why we're struggling, but we know that something doesn't feel right.

As I went through the motions of my busy daily life, a gnawing ache began to claw its way to the surface. A longing that refused to be ignored. At first, I brushed it aside with the excuse that I was just tired, overextended, simply overwhelmed with the demands of life. I vowed to sleep more, eat healthier foods and practice stress reduction methods. Since I was also raising toddlers, that didn't go very well!

The ache grew stronger and I realized that a deep part of me felt lost. I didn't seem to belong anywhere. Even when surrounded by family and friends, loneliness pressed on my chest like a rock. Worst of all, I felt restless and uncomfortable in my own home.

This unsettled longing was not new. It had been part of my life since childhood. When I lived in my parents' home, I couldn't wait for the day when I could move out and live on my own. Newly married, I eagerly set up my first household in a rented mobile home, but things still didn't feel right. I decided that owning my own home would ease the inner longing and began saving for a down payment.

Unlocking the door to our very own fixer-upper, I dreamed of how satisfied I would feel when we finished the lengthy list of renovations. Still, the restless ache persisted. When we moved to a grand old house in the Adirondack mountains, I threw myself into creating another home and opening a bed and breakfast. Making people feel "at home away from home" became my daily job and I was very good at it. Yet, I still felt lost in my own space … restless, lonely, distracted and irritable.

I had gained my independence, owned my own home, completed umpteen improvement projects, moved to an even larger home and designed a beautiful lodging space. Yet I still didn't feel satisfied. Our family enjoyed many wonderful moments, but we also dealt with exhaustion, stress, anger and depression. Despite my best efforts, many days our home felt more like a battlefield than a sanctuary.

My heart felt raw from my lifelong struggle with abandonment, fear and depression. My adopted children carried their own burdens and deserved a mother who could be a reassuring source of strength and joy. We all desperately needed a safe and healing home.

My longing for home led me to search for answers. Thankfully, that search led me to discover a beautiful way of life with the power to transform even a crazy, chaotic household into a haven. This way of life I now call Blessing.

Soul Questions

When it comes to renovating or redecorating your home, the available resources seem limitless. Books, magazines, blogs, webinars, YouTube videos, and TV shows offer instructions for everything from plumbing to painting to "porcelainizing" your tub! You can find 40,500,000 websites just to help you build a backyard grill pit (yep – I googled it).

But where are the tutorials for rehabbing the less-than-lovely areas of our lives? Who has a solution for the weary mom staring at yet another mountain of dirty laundry while her baby clings to her leg? What about the single person facing another long weekend in an echoing apartment? Or the couple whose seething irritation erupts into a fight almost nightly? Where do you turn when you feel restless, disillusioned and lonely? When you can't fall asleep without a drink? When you don't feel at home anywhere – not even in your own home?

Very few people talk honestly about the real lives that take place within the walls of their home. Since we've become masters at avoiding these uncomfortable topics, most of us think that we're struggling alone. We fear that somehow everyone else has figured out how to do life and we are the stray weirdo who just can't seem to get it together.

One evening when my children were young, we invited about a dozen friends for dinner. What was I thinking, you ask? Remember that I was still playing the strong, capable superwoman role. Midway through the evening, I couldn't keep up the charade. My head pounded. My chest felt so heavy that I could barely breathe. The chatter of voices grated on my exhausted nerves. I was in real danger of melting down on the spot.

Desperate for a quiet moment, I escaped to my basement.

Now it should be noted that this basement was not the cozy, family room version with overstuffed couches and a pool table. Hand-dug by a previous owner, it featured limestone rocks jutting from dirt walls, scary-big spiders lurking in corners and damp puddles on the concrete where water seeped in. In other words, this was the last place someone would go to hang out unless they felt hopeless.

Too tired to even stand, I curled up on a pile of dirty laundry. I couldn't pretend to be strong anymore. I felt too drained and broken to talk, think or meet one more person's expectation. Lying in the darkness, I listened to the footsteps and laughter of my family and dinner guests overhead. A full-blown party was underway and the hostess (me) was MIA. Almost an hour passed as I dozed on and off. Each time I faded back into reality, I felt amazed that no one had come looking for me. A sad sort of amazed but not really surprised.

For months, my struggle with exhaustion, depression and anxiety seemed invisible to others. I worked incredibly hard to keep everything together while secretly hoping someone would notice my pain and help me. I even dropped a few hints around my closest friends – little tests to see if anyone could see or hear me.

Nope.

As long as the show went on, and I kept doing all of the "right" things, everyone seemed content to ignore the pain in my eyes.

Looking back, I believe that my friends and family chose not to see. Not because they didn't care, but because they were afraid. Afraid that allowing me to lower my "successful, busy mom" mask might also dislodge the carefully constructed images they held up to the world. Afraid that listening to my struggles might force them to face their own painful questions.

Do I belong?

Am I safe?

Does my story matter?

As I wrestled with these questions in my own life, suddenly I began to see and hear them everywhere. I still felt alone because no one talked about their struggles, but it became apparent that all of us were asking these soul questions every day. From our interactions to our priorities to our attitudes, almost everything we did as humans seemed designed to answer one or more of these questions.

> Our search for belonging,
> safety and significance can
> be traced back to the place
> where we received
> the first answers to our
> soul questions ... Home.

The sights, sounds and sensations you recalled a few moments ago provide important clues to your connection to home. Did you feel that you belonged? Did you feel safe? Did you feel that you mattered? If you grew up in a secure and loving home, your earliest soul questions were answered with a reassuring YES. But if your memories reverberate with anger, stress, abuse or fear, you have most likely internalized a painful NO. If you're like me, you remember a combination of times when you felt loved and secure and other times when you felt abandoned and alone.

When it comes to building our own homes as adults, our memories guide us more than we realize. We work to create a home that is either *like* the one we grew up in or *better than* what we experienced as a child. No matter how old we are or how much success we've enjoyed, we still want to know where we belong, if we're safe and most of all, we really want to know that we matter.

Our soul questions motivate and drive our lives. The good news is that the very questions that rattle and unsettle us also lead us to the answers.

Your True Home

From mansions to mobile homes, from high rises to huts, from cottages by the sea to college dorms, we all feel the urge to carve out our own special place on the planet. The instinct to create a home is primal and powerful. Take an ordinary apartment complex with row upon row of identical concrete boxes. If you move 100 different people into these spaces, by sundown, each one will have made their home uniquely theirs. One apartment blooms with an eclectic collection of colorful items from around the world while the one next door boasts a modern minimalist palette of black, white and chrome.

We gather colors, fabrics and belongings around ourselves much as a bird feathers its nest. But these items only tell part of the story.

Home holds such power because it resonates with something deep inside. In the core of your being, an ancient knowing guides your entire human experience. From the moment of your first breath until your last, you are a traveler on a beautiful journey. A journey that began and ends with home.

Creating a true home
requires you to connect to
your spirit's home — the place
where your story actually begins.

You entered this adventure called life at an exact moment in time. On your birth day, you arrived on planet earth and immediately began to collect a treasure trove of memories. As you interact with your surroundings through your five senses, each sight, smell, taste, word and experience creates an imprint in your brain, forming a biological archive of your physical history.

But you are more than skin, bones, organs and blood vessels.

Housed inside the physical structure of your body is an essence that cannot be experienced through the five senses. An invisible, indestructible energy animates your body and makes you ALIVE. This inner essence enables you to move, think, feel, create, decide and interpret your life. Without this life force, your body would be an empty, motionless shell.

This hidden part of you is your spirit. The real YOU.

Now please don't get squirmy on me. I can hear some of you saying, "Whoa! Don't go there. I'm not a spiritual person."

Before you roll your eyes and close the book, consider that you experience and operate in this unseen realm all the time. Thoughts. Emotions. Dreams. Imagination. Deja vu. Instinct. Passions. Values. Intuition. None of these are tangible and yet you easily accept them as real. You can't see or hold or smell your personality, but you know that you have one. Spiritual concepts are not weird or spooky. They are simply expressions of the non-physical, unseen part of you – the world of your spirit.

While you learned about the birds and bees at a young age, you may not have given much thought to how your spirit arrived in your body. The miracle of biological reproduction formed your physical body, resulting in the day of your birth. But where is the birthplace of your spirit?

Scientists have tried for centuries to dissect the mystery of the spirit. In laboratories around the world, they've genetically engineered, cloned and created new physical bodies. Despite diligent effort, no one has been able to isolate, identify or insert a spirit into any of these experiments. LIFE comes from another realm. In order to understand the unseen life force within us, we must be willing to explore the world we cannot know with our physical senses.

Your spirit, the life force within you, existed before your human journey began and will continue on after your body returns to dust. As French philosopher, Pierre Teilhard de Chardin wrote, *"We are not human beings having a spiritual experience. **We are spiritual beings having a human experience.**"*

11

Spiritual traditions teach that we come to earth with a distinct purpose, a divine calling, a lesson we are to learn or a message that we are to deliver. I've always been intrigued by the scripture passage where God tells the prophet Jeremiah, *"Before I formed you in the womb, I knew you, before you were born, I set you apart. I appointed you as a prophet to the nations."* [1]

As a spirit, you existed in a place of infinite Love where you never questioned your worth or experienced a need. You knew nothing of pain, struggle or defeat. The blessings of beauty, peace, joy and love surrounded you. Even before your birth, you were known. You were set apart. And when the time was right, you arrived from this beautiful beyond, perfectly designed for a role that only you can play.

Born into this exact time and place in history, your spirit began to have a human experience.

Culture Shock

I 've been a devoted royal watcher since Princess Diana stole my 12-year-old heart, so you'll have to forgive me for this next analogy. Imagine if little Prince George, heir to the British throne, were suddenly plucked from the luxury and safety of Kensington Palace and plopped in the middle of a cornfield in Kansas. Or a refugee camp in Syria. Or a jungle village in the Amazon. Or a cul-de-sac in New Jersey.

At first, our little prince would be frightened, confused, maybe even angry. He would desperately long to go home. But in time, he would adjust to his new surroundings, learning the new rules and ways of life in the country, the camp, the jungle or his new suburban school. He would settle into a new daily routine, experience new adventures and even make new friends. Slowly, the memories of his formerly privileged life would fade. But not completely. When he least expected it, a nameless nostalgia would nudge him. In quiet moments, he would hear an inner echo of trumpets and pageantry.

A part of him would never fully forget that he was once a prince.

The culture shock that Prince George feels in our story doesn't begin to compare to the trauma of what you've experienced! Since the moment of your birth, you've encountered pain, disappointment, injustice and failure – all quite foreign and frightening to your spirit. (You quite possibly spent the first seconds of your life being spanked by a well-intentioned doctor!)

Despite the jarring aspects of your new reality, like Prince George, you've adapted well. You've learned to embrace the beauty, adventure, friendship and fun of your human experience. Over time, the memory of your once-perfect home has faded from your consciousness. But not completely. Deep inside, you hear the echoes from another time and place. Even your most beautiful moments feel haunted by a twinge of longing.

A part of you still remembers.

The Power of Remembering

B iting into a concord grape immediately transports me to my eight-year-old self, standing barefoot in the grass at my grandmother's house and plucking sun-warmed grapes from her vines. The sound of popcorn popping reminds me of my dad. I can't see a pansy without remembering my mom's excitement each spring when she planted her "happy flowers."

Even though I'm now a full-fledged grown up with a home of my own, it only takes a smell, a taste or a song on the radio to suddenly interrupt my life with the bittersweet nudge of nostalgia. I am no longer that barefoot girl, but she is undeniably a part of who I am today. During the best and worst moments of my life, I find myself yearning for what feels familiar and safe.

And so do you. You just may not have thought of it that way.

As long as you live in human form, you will never fully shake the ache. In hard times, you find yourself flaring with anger, frustration and fear that seems out of proportion for what you're experiencing. Even your best moments feel a little empty - as if something is still "off."

If you don't understand what's happening, you may feel like something is very wrong with you. You may work longer hours, accumulate more things, take splashier vacations and fill your days with non-stop activity. Or you may shut down and sedate yourself against the pain with drugs, alcohol, overeating, shopping and endless Netflix marathons. You may quit your job, divorce your wife, visit a therapist, attend church, join AA. If you're like most people, you will do whatever it takes to escape the discomfort of your humanity. This is what we do.

We create lives that silence the ache. The very ache that is meant to guide us home.

Please hear me, dear one. There is nothing wrong with you! The ache, the longing, the angst ... all of the feelings that you try so hard to suppress ... are actually signs that something is beautifully, eternally RIGHT. In those moments, your spirit is reaching out for the answers to your soul questions. Your spirit is remembering home.

You are lonely because you once knew complete belonging.

You are sad because you once knew perfect joy.

You are angry because you once knew a world where everyone was loved.

You are unsatisfied because you once possessed wealth that could not be measured.

You are a hot mess because you are HOMESICK!

Feeling homesick isn't a bad thing. In fact, longing for home means that you have experienced a place where you feel safe, comfortable and nurtured. The desires that burn within you are not designed to make you miserable, but to gently, continually turn your heart toward home. Like a love note slipped into a child's lunchbox or a loved one's luggage, moments of beauty, joy and abundance are sprinkled all over your life so that home will never be far from your mind. The resulting ache urges you to reach out, to spiritually "call home" now and then!

When you delight in something beautiful or experience intense joy, you feel the pang of remembering even greater beauty and joy. When the heartache and harshness of this broken world slap you in the face, the sting carries with it the deep awareness that you deserve better. You know instinctively that there is a place where these evils do not exist.

Home calls to you through
the hard times
and whispers even in your
happiest moments.

The longing can never be soothed by buying a new couch, repainting the bathroom or installing a hot tub. The only solution is to return "home" by reconnecting to the truth that your spirit already knows:

You belong

You are always safe

Your story absolutely matters!

Breathed into this world by
Spirit itself, your life is a beautiful
remembering — a journey home.

I love the quote from Ram Dass, "We are all just walking each other home." You are not alone on your journey. Neither am I. This book is part of my walking with you. And I sincerely thank you for walking with me.

Learning to Listen

As if juggling work, family, home renovations and inner turmoil wasn't enough, our well became severely contaminated with ecoli. We thought we had the stomach bug from hell as our entire family battled crippling nausea and other unpleasant side effects for several months. By the time a routine water test revealed the cause, I had become seriously sick. Each day felt like a marathon of trying to care for my responsibilities between waves of stomach cramps and weakness that forced me to lie down almost hourly.

My first few trips to the doctor resulted in a kitchen counter full of prescriptions designed to alleviate my symptoms. I obediently swallowed pills to calm my nausea, applied steroid cream to soothe my peeling skin and even considered filling the prescription for anti-depressants that the doctor eagerly pressed into my hand. But after a few months, I still felt lousy and kept developing new symptoms. (Have you ever read the disclaimers on those drug information sheets?!)

In desperation, I made an appointment to visit a naturopathic clinic recommended by a friend. The first clue that this doctor was different came when he didn't hand me a lengthy intake form. In fact, he stopped me mid-sentence when I tried to explain my medical history and shudder-worthy symptoms. Patting the table, he said, "Go ahead and lie down. Your body will tell me what's wrong."

Say what? The skeptic in me wanted to scamper out of his office, but I was horribly sick and running out of options. So I laid down on the table, closed my eyes, whispered a prayer that I wouldn't get sucked into a cult and let him "listen" to my body. Thus began a two-year journey that opened my eyes to a whole new kind of healing.

This doctor saw me as more than just a body with mechanical parts that could break down. He understood that I possessed an inner world of energy, emotion, intuition and wisdom. Rather than seeing my symptoms as inconveniences to be swiftly dispatched, he followed their clues to find the root causes. I received a thorough education on how the foods I ate, the thoughts I thought and the emotions that surged through my body all played a role in both my illness and my healing.

While I had always taken care of my body and nurtured a strong spiritual life, I had viewed these as two completely separate practices. I now understood for the first time that my body and spirit were intricately linked in a beautiful, lifelong dance. By nurturing both the inner and outer worlds of my body, I began to heal.

Thinking like a holistic doctor, I began to see my whole life differently. Stress, exhaustion and pain were not enemies to be eliminated, silenced or ignored. They were messengers. Friends really. When I followed their clues, they led me right to the places in my life that needed healing.

What a relief to realize that I was not the hopeless mess I'd feared I was! As Glennon Doyle puts it, I was a "deeply feeling person in a messy world."[2] My life was still crazy and busy and overwhelming, but a cautious excitement began to mingle with my helplessness.

The very things that caused me pain now appeared to be portals through which I could find healing.

Maybe I wasn't failing at life after all. Maybe I had simply forgotten who I was and where I came from. My spirit was starving for the comfort, safety and blessing of its home. By listening to these inner longings, I slowly began to create a home that nurtured both my body and spirit.

Sacred Space

Have you ever walked into a room and immediately sensed the mood? Perhaps the air felt thick with irritation, heaviness or tension that you "could cut with a knife." Maybe you've been home alone and suddenly felt unexplained goosebumps or a sense of being watched. On a more pleasant note, you've experienced a tingle of excitement in the air, the cozy warmth of a welcoming space or the intimacy of sitting next to someone and feeling connected without needing to say a word.

All of these sensations are possible because the atmosphere around you is not an empty vacuum. Our entire world is composed of both seen and unseen. Inner and outer. Body and spirit.

Just as the framework of your skin and bones houses the truest part of you, your home's physical structure of brick, stone and glass contain a sacred space that hums and crackles with invisible but measurable waves of energy and LIFE. This unseen world is just as real as the walls and furniture that you can touch and see.

> The spirit of your home
> transforms it from an
> empty shell into a vibrant,
> interactive environment.

In the past few years, concepts like self-care, consciousness, mindfulness, reflection and meditation have moved from their isolated niches into mainstream awareness. A booming wellness industry offers countless self-help books and seminars held in schools, churches, workplaces and community centers. Support groups and online forums provide a safe place for us to share our struggles about everything from mom guilt to addiction to broken hearts. As a society, we're finally figuring out that our mental and emotional health requires the same love and attention as our physical bodies.

It is time to bring this same attention to the sacred space of our homes. We know how to cook, clean, mow the grass and do the laundry. But we've missed some very key lessons. Few of us have been taught:

- what to do when the kids (or you!) meltdown in frustration
- how to clear the heaviness in the air after a negative neighbor visits
- how to protect and restore our bodies and spirits from rampant stress and exhaustion
- what causes the nightmares that wake us in a cold sweat
- how to shift our low-grade sadness to embracing more joy
- how to create a space that honors and heals our deepest hurts
- how to really support a loved one who is struggling

Our preparation for true home-making falls woefully short. Exactly how DO you care for the unseen part of your home?

The answer is surprisingly, refreshingly simple.

When I was sick, my healing involved two clear strategies. First, the doctor focused on a careful detoxing from the ecoli that saturated my body. Then we nourished my body with healing supplements and foods. In simple terms, cleaning out the junk and replacing it with the good stuff. It turns out that this is also an excellent formula for creating a healthy home!

The rest of this book will thoroughly examine these two aspects of creating a home for your body and spirit. In the Cleansing section, you will learn how to remove the negative, toxic influences that contaminate your home's atmosphere. Then the Blessing section will guide you in creating a beautiful lifestyle that replenishes the cleaned-out space with the lovely qualities that your spirit remembers and longs to experience again.

Please know that there is nothing mysterious, frightening or difficult about any of this. Once you understand the process, caring for your home's sacred space will feel as natural as taking out the trash, flossing your teeth or cooking a healthy dinner for your family.

It's time to begin creating a sanctuary where your body and spirit can rest and reconnect to your true home. But first, you must take one very significant and powerful step.

Moving In

D o you remember the moment you received the keys to your home? Whether you were renting, buying or bumming your buddy's back bedroom, opening that door for the first time signaled a fresh beginning. With pride, you inserted the key in the lock, took a deep breath and went in to claim your territory! You felt the thrill of possibility as you carried your belongings across the threshold into your very own small piece of the planet.

Having a place to call home meets a fundamental human desire. No one in their right mind would go to the effort of finding a home, signing the paperwork, making monthly payments and then never bother to move in! Imagine letting your home sit empty with doors and windows open to wind and rain, creepy critters or the town drunk. Or even more disgusting, picture setting up house in the middle of the last owner's clutter and leftover trash.

Of course, you would never do any of these things!

And yet when you don't consciously "move in" to the unseen part of your home, this is precisely what you do. You leave your spiritual space unclaimed. Through unguarded openings, you allow outside influences and energies to enter and control the atmosphere of your home. Your body occupies the physical space, but your spirit feels like an intruder. No wonder you feel unsettled, uneasy and not fully at home.

When you don't clear your home's sacred space, you live surrounded by the energetic remnants of someone else's life.

Signing your name on a lease or deed brings certain rights and responsibilities. You receive the power to choose who lives with you, the color scheme, the music that's played, what food is in the fridge and how late you stay up at night. As long as you're obeying the law and respecting your neighbors, you can live the lifestyle you want. You have paid for the privilege to enjoy and control your space.

Moving into the sacred space of your home empowers you to make that space yours as well. You get to decide what influences may enter your home, what energy or attitude is allowed to dominate, and what lifestyle will be embraced in that space. Such important decisions shouldn't be left to chance, and yet too often, they are!

What if you don't own your home? Do the same rights apply if you're renting an apartment or living with a friend or relative?

Yes! Remember that everything has a physical and spiritual aspect. Even buildings. Each home has a legal, physical owner and a spiritual owner. Sometimes they are the same, but often they are two different entities. The building you live in may be legally owned by a bank or a landlord, but once the contract is signed and the key is placed in your hand, you are charged with the right and responsibility to protect and nurture that space – not only physically, but also spiritually.

> ## Creating a home that honors both body and spirit may be the most significant work you will ever do on this earth.

If you are like most people, you spend a great deal of time and energy acquiring and maintaining your belongings. You wash the dishes, sweep the floor, fold the laundry (maybe!), mow the grass, fill the car with gas. The tasks seem endless and yet you are investing all of this effort into physical possessions that can be lost, broken, or stolen. Your couch, your fridge, your car and even your body can be destroyed by disaster or disease.

The only untouchable part of you is the unseen you – your

spirit, your courage, your dreams, your faith, hope and love. How much time do you spend caring for your inner world or consciously maintaining the atmosphere of your home? Do you give it even five minutes a day?

You and your loved ones are spirits having a human experience. In your own ways, each of you is asking soul questions, feeling the restless ache and hearing echoes from your true home. What you need cannot be satisfied through a bigger paycheck or better stuff. Invest your time and energy in what truly matters - the things that cannot be destroyed. Your home could burn to the ground tomorrow, but the memories, emotions and connections made within those walls will live on eternally.

No one else can fill the role of caretaker for your home's sacred space. This is your work. Sacred work. It's time to move in and make your home a Blessed Home! Just as receiving the keys to your physical home brought a tingle of anticipation and hope, let today represent that same fresh start for your home's sacred space.

Now go ahead and step over that threshold!

Moving In Ceremony

Remember that even if you are not the legal owner of your home, you can still spiritually claim your space. Hold the keys to your home, apartment or dorm room in your hand and make the following declaration thoughtfully and with confidence. (Substitute the word "we" if you are doing this with a partner)

I give sincere thanks for this home and joyfully receive the gift of a space to call my own. When I accepted this key, I promised to live in and care for this home. In the same way, I now consciously move into the sacred, unseen space within these walls. I acknowledge my role as the spiritual owner of this home and promise to protect, nurture and bless this space. It is an honor to create a home for both body and spirit - for myself (and my family). For as long as I live in this home, I will fulfill this role to the best of my ability. May it be so.

Summary of Home Section

1. Home is the soil into which you are planted. Creating a home may be the single most important thing we do as humans

2. We spend billions annually on home goods, yet many of us struggle to feel "at home." We feel exhausted, stressed and empty inside.

3. Our childhood home provides the first answers to our soul questions. *Do I belong? Am I safe? Does my story matter?* Most of our adult life is spent continuing to seek the answers.

4. Your spirit is ageless and boundless. You came from a place of pure Love and perfection. You are a spiritual being having a human experience. From the moment of your first breath until your last, you are on a beautiful journey toward home.

5. Even though you've adjusted to the imperfections of this physical world, you hear echoes from another time and place. No matter how good things are in your life, something still feels slightly "off." Even your most beautiful moments feel haunted by a faint longing.

6. Your spirit remembers home. The homesickness (which comes disguised as grief, anger, depression, exhaustion) is a gift intended to gently, continually turn your heart toward your true home.

7. When you learn to listen to your body and spirit, you realize that stress, exhaustion and pain are not enemies to be covered or silenced or ignored. They are messengers that will lead you to the places in your home that need healing.

8. Just as you are both body and spirit, so is your home. Caring for it involves both Cleansing (removing what you don't want) and Blessing (putting in what you do want.)

9. Consciously moving into the sacred space of your home empowers you to make that space truly yours. You have the right to decide what influences, energies or attitudes are allowed to dominate the atmosphere.

Let no sadness come
through this gate.
Let no trouble come to
this dwelling.

Let no fear come
through this door.
Let no conflict be in
this place.

Let this home be filled
with the blessing of joy
and peace.

JEWISH BLESSING

PART 2

Cleansing

Life Gets Messy

The smell began as a whiff barely dancing at the edges of my consciousness as I walked through the upstairs hallway. *Probably one of the kids' dirty socks,* I thought. The next day, an even stronger odor greeted me and I made a mental note to look for the offending sock. As usual, life was busy and a few days passed. Now my husband began noticing the smell. *Something stinks upstairs!* It was time to get serious about finding the source of the smell.

Over the next week, we carried out our mission by washing all of the dirty laundry, sprinkling baking soda on the carpet, searching under beds and behind dressers. We found nothing. Meanwhile, the smell grew to a stench so powerful we could hardly breathe. The August heat certainly made matters worse!

Finally, we determined that the smell seemed strongest near a little-used linen closet in our back hallway. My husband opened the door and stared at the shelves of extra bedding and outgrown clothing. *A mouse must have died in here.* With a stronger stomach than I possessed, he began the tedious job of digging through each bag and box. Almost an hour later, he dragged a large garbage bag down the stairs, wearing an expression of horrified disgust.

Mid-way through the school year, my daughter, always a lover of home-packed lunches, suddenly noticed that the majority of her friends were now buying lunch. Not wanting to appear uncool but also not wanting upset us, she continued to take her packed lunch to school every day. After school, she came home and headed straight upstairs where she buried her untouched lunch deep in the bowels of this obscure closet. Day after day. Month after month. Until the school year ended in June. It was now AUGUST and my husband had unearthed dozens of bags of rotting fruit, molding bread and slimy lunch meat.

On the surface, our home looked clean and lovely, but hidden in a place we couldn't see, a mess festered. A mess that would eventually seep into our daily life!

As humans, we usually choose to avoid things that are difficult, frightening or just plain unsavory. We hope that if we keep things looking good on the outside, whatever lurks underneath will magically fade away. This explains why we make appointments to get our hair and nails done but never find the time to schedule a mammogram! Or book a holiday cruise instead of talking things through with our mother-in-law. Or open a new credit card rather than curb our spending addiction. Or spend thousands on home renovations that could have been invested in couples therapy.

Too often, we live by these philosophies:

"What you don't know can't hurt you."

"Ignorance is bliss."

"Ignore something long enough and it will go away."

Sometimes we get lucky and the thing we dread does disappear. But rarely. Most messes don't go away. Like a cancer growing quietly day after day, our hidden struggles multiply until we can no longer pretend them into submission. Every day that we spend simply treating symptoms instead of finding the real issue is another wasted day. Another day where we smile and say we're fine while our heart feels heavy. Another day lost to pain and struggle instead of Blessing.

Hidden messes always find a way to seep into our lives – toying with our thoughts and emotions, shaping our interactions with others and even impacting our physical health. Nowhere is this truer than in our homes. We can fake our way through the surface interactions of work, carpool and even church, but home is where life gets real!

The atmosphere within a home literally reverberates with the stories of the people who live in it.

The older the home, the more history is held within the walls. Decades pass. Good times and hard times. People coming and going. Angry moments. Loving moments. The home collects more and more of the energetic residue of life. Over time, a home filled with laughter will develop a very different atmosphere than a home that has witnessed decades of angry words.

Because these concepts can feel surreal, I like to use the analogy of dirt and cleansing. We're all familiar with the need to clean our homes regularly. There's no avoiding the fact that life is messy!

Every time you come through the door of your home, you carry some of the world's dust and grime in with you. Inside, you create more messes. Cooking creates scraps and greasy dishes. Every night, you toss your worn clothing in the hamper or on the floor depending on your personality. From soap rings in the tub to mail piles on the counter, a "lived-in" home collects dirt and clutter.

Your unseen world also collects dirt and clutter. Every person who enters a home, even for a brief visit, leaves behind traces of their personal history and energy. If you could see the spiritual dirt that surrounds you, most likely you would be shocked. You would never allow such grimy conditions to exist in your physical home, and yet you innocently live your life surrounded by the emotional residue of generations of others.

No more! Now that you've moved into the sacred space of your home, you need to do what any good home-owner would do: give the place a good scrubbing and then fill it up with beautiful and useful things.

First the Cleansing, then the Blessing.

In the chapters ahead, you will learn to recognize the various kinds of spiritual dirt present in your home and how to clean each one. (No need to use a blow torch when a simple dust cloth will do!)

You will listen to the *messages* in the messes, using them to identify the areas that need the most Blessing. In the same way that you dust, sweep, sort and organize to keep your physical home in top shape, you will develop simple routines to maintain the sacred space of your home.

Go ahead ... grab your spiritual scrub bucket and let's get to work! Trust me, things will feel a lot better when you're done.

Dust

When the late afternoon sunlight slants through the window, what do you see? Millions of tiny dust particles dancing in the rays. Without question, dust is the most common household dirt. Wood, earth, rock, cloth and even our bodies break down into the little particles that we call dust. Dust travels in and out with you, sticking to your shoes, riding on your clothes, wafting through open doors and windows. Even clean freaks live surrounded by dust every moment of every day. Unless you have asthma or a severe allergy, you casually accept dust as part of life and don't pay it much attention until you notice that you can write your name on the furniture.

Now at this point, please note that you do not panic. In fact, I'm pretty sure that no one has ever run screaming from a room because they spotted dust. You understand that dust is not serious or dangerous, so you calmly reach for a cloth and wipe it away. Even though dust returns again and again, you still don't despair or freak out. You know that you can simply wipe it away again.

What is the spiritual equivalent of dust? What do the invisible parts of our world break down into? What exists everywhere and in everything - so common that we live surrounded by it and barely notice? So easily cleared that we do not need to worry?

The answer is energy.

While physical objects break down into visible dust, the invisible substance that forms our universe is energy. From books to waterfalls to pumpkins to skyscrapers to dolphins to the rhythm of your heart, everything is composed of this living, vibrating, intelligent substance. Energy is the animating "spirit" that exists within the "body" of all that we see.

Although you may not give much thought to energy's movement around us, you experience its reality every day in many tangible ways.

Invisible communication signals allow you to watch your favorite TV show, listen to music while you jog and zip text messages around the world in milliseconds. Microwaves utilize radio waves at specific frequencies to agitate the water molecules in last night's leftovers, resulting in heat. If you visit the ER with chest pains, doctors will analyze the electrical waves of your heart using an EKG. Depression and addictions can be treated using positive and negative stimuli controlled by your brainwaves, a process known as neurofeedback. Sound waves carry the song of a bird, the laughter of a baby and the crescendo of a symphony to your ears. All of these everyday "miracles" are made possible by the unseen dust of the universe – energy.

Energy is in constant motion – changing, creating and communicating. Scientists measure energy's motion by vibration. The faster the vibration, the harder the substance – like a table or a rock. Softer objects, like your flesh or water, vibrate very slowly.

Your body responds to the ever-changing environment around you with a complex system of measurable reactions. Neurons fire. Chemicals release. Organs respond. Moods change. Thoughts form. Cells regenerate. At the physical, cellular level, your body changes so rapidly that you are literally not the same person you were yesterday or even five seconds ago. Each experience triggers thousands of biological and emotional reactions in your body. Dr. Bruce Lipton tells us that through these responses and the beliefs you form as a result, "you rewrite the chemistry of your body."[3]

At the spiritual, energetic level, you are also a responsive being with infinite possibilities. As you constantly assess, evaluate, react and readjust to the stimuli around you, your body's reactions change the energetic vibration of your body. All of this happens so frequently and easily that you are seldom aware of the shifts.

After a happy or meaningful experience, your body's energy vibrates at a measurably higher frequency. You've probably heard self-help teachers speak of "raising your vibration" as a way to feel lighter and more positive. If you're feeling frightened or angry, your vibration slows to a lower frequency, resulting in a heavy, weighty sensation.

Daily Dust

From morning to night, your body and spirit engage in a constant dance of cause and effect. If you wake early, go for a run, wear a cute outfit and car dance to happy music on your drive to work, your brain releases cascades of positive chemicals and hormones that wash through every cell in your body. You will stand straighter, smile more and walk with a bounce in your step. Everyone around you will sense that you're having a good day.

However, if you oversleep, dash out the door without showering, gobble down a doughnut from the gas station and have a fender-bender in the parking lot, you'll be flooded with a completely different set of cellular and energetic reactions.

Think of how many emotions you feel in one day. Joy. Depression. Irritation. Amusement. Self-confidence. Shame. Contentment. Loneliness. From moment to moment, thousands of invisible, internal reactions ebb and flow in direct response to your choices and experiences. These biological rhythms and energetic vibrations ripple through your body and beyond, radiating into the atmosphere around you.

> Like the frequencies of a radio station, you literally broadcast the story of your life in a way that others can "hear" without you saying a word.

Now here is where things get interesting! Everyone you meet is broadcasting their story too. Like it or not, you have to deal with the energy of your boss, your friend, your partner, your children – even the Starbucks barista. Each person you encounter is engaged in their own version of the cause and effect dance, sending out unseen signals that you can sense. Your energy mingles and clashes and interacts and aligns with the energy of those around you, causing even more biological responses and vibrational waves.

In other words, you live surrounded by a lot of energetic dust!

When you come home from work, a play date at the park or the doctor's office, you carry the residue of your interactions into your home. Like dust on your shoes, whatever energy has "stuck" to you throughout the day now begins to scatter throughout your unseen, sacred space. Filtering from your boss to you to your dog. Although you cannot see energy dancing in the afternoon light, it is just as real as the dust gathering on your mantel.

With all of this energetic dust flying around, it would seem that we would experience mass chaos. But our universe operates beautifully and systematically. Instead of a discordant clash of insanity, vibrations seek other similar vibrations and group together, creating order.

Tuning forks clearly demonstrate this reality. When one tuning fork is struck, a second tuning fork begins to resonate at the same pitch. An invisible sound wave has traveled across the room and communicated with the receptive tuning fork. In the same way, your energy vibrates through the atmosphere, seeking to align with what "resonates" most closely to your own vibration.

We feel most comfortable with people who vibrate at or near the same energy frequency as we do.

You've heard the sayings "birds of a feather flock together" and "misery loves company." This explains why you feel drawn to one person and repelled by another. If you are an introvert, you vibrate a quieter, calmer energy and feel overwhelmed by loud, boisterous life-of-the-party types. If you are low-energy in the morning, you may feel like punching the cheery coworker who whistles around the office. Sometimes you'll meet a new acquaintance and "click right away" while other people will mysteriously "rub you the wrong way." It all has to do with your vibration. You are constantly seeking to align with or retreat from the other person's energy.

The Battle of the Vibes

So what happens when you encounter a conflicting vibration? Who wins?

Amazingly, once a vibration begins, it expands like ripples in a pond, seeking and attracting every similar energy toward itself. As the vibration broadcasts its energy outward, weaker energies in the vicinity begin to tune to the stronger frequency, causing it to gather even more strength. The negative or positive energy spreads from one object or person to another. This phenomenon will continue until the vibration encounters a stronger one that overpowers it and causes it to change. A persistent, dominant energy always shifts the atmosphere around it as less powerful vibrations are drawn into alignment, tuning to the dominant vibe.

You've already experienced this reality. One grumpy coworker puts a damper on an entire office. The jovial cashier lifts the spirits of everyone in his checkout line. You feel frazzled after just a few moments with a highly stressed person. In each case, these people affect you because they are vibrating more strongly than you. Or perhaps you are the dominant vibration, causing those around you to mirror what you're feeling. If you can walk into a room and immediately command attention and respect, you carry a very strong energy.

Nowhere is the battle of the vibes more evident than in the safety and intimacy of home. Someone sets the tone for your home. Is it you? Your partner? A child?

Pay attention to how the energy shifts when dad comes in the door. Or when a certain child gets home from school. Whoever emits the strongest "signal" will always shift the atmosphere as the others begin to resonate with their energy. Over and over, I've seen this happen in my home. One child begins to whine, another joins in and soon even the dog is thumping her water bowl in frustration. Or someone shares a funny video, laughing hysterically, and soon we're all feeling silly and light-hearted. When you see one person's mood spreading to another and another, you are witnessing firsthand how a dominant vibration tunes the others to itself. "Mama ain't happy, ain't nobody happy" is a real thing!

The consistent dominant energy of your home literally shapes the lives of those who live there.

Imagine an environment that is routinely filled with love, laughter and encouragement. Even in the quiet moments, the vibrations of joy and love continue to resonate within its walls. Now imagine living surrounded by a dominant energy of anger, sarcasm, disrespect or even abuse. The very air crackles with tension and stress, causing stomachs to knot, muscles to tense and blood pressures to rise.

Taking control of the energy of your home will be one of your most important tasks as the spiritual caretaker for your home. What do you think is the dominant energy? Who is setting the tone? Are your family members joyful, cooperative and loving? I hope so! But if you notice a lot of exhaustion, bickering or loneliness, chances are high that you're living in a build-up of negative energy.

You need not panic. Like household dust, energy is not dangerous. Both are a normal part of life – one is visible and the other is not. Whether you're dealing with a few flecks of energetic dust or rolling dust bunnies, the solution is the same: simply wipe away the dust you don't want. You can shift the atmosphere of your home by interrupting the ripples of negative energy and consciously creating a stronger, dominant vibration that is more in "tune" with the energy you desire in your home.

Dusting Your Sacred Space

Growing up, our home ran on a weekly cleaning schedule. Laundry was always done on Tuesday, ironing on Wednesday, shopping on Thursday. For some reason, I don't remember Monday or Friday, but I do recall spending every Saturday morning of my childhood with a dust cloth in my hand. My mother was onto something. Her consistent routines prevented the dirt in our home from getting out of hand.

Clearing your sacred space of negative energy should be a routine part of your daily (or at least weekly) routine. Here are some simple ways to dust away energy that doesn't belong in your home.

- Shake it Off – I'm an empath – meaning that I easily pick up on others' emotions or vibes. When I start feeling anxious or sad or irritable, I've learned to stop and ask, "Is something actually wrong here?" Nine times out of ten, my own life is just fine! I'm merely sneezing on someone else's dust. Even when it comes to the struggles of your child or spouse, it's important that you don't align with their vibe and thereby increase it. You can be loving and supportive without carrying another person's stress or pain. Several times a day, pay attention to the dust that's settling on you. Take a moment to consciously dust yourself. Dance to a few bars of a cheery song with a theme of "let it go" or "shake it off." A good friend of mine literally brushes her hands over her shoulders, arms, chest, sides and legs. In a few swift movements, she symbolically brushes away the dust of unwanted emotional energy. Every time you shower or wash your hands, envision the water rinsing off any unpleasant energetic residue from your day.
- Cancel Negative Thoughts and Words – We all have certain phrases that we've grown up hearing. Over and over, they cycle through our mind and we often speak them. *"This*

place is a mess." "Nobody ever helps around here." "I'm exhausted." "I can't live like this anymore." "With my luck ..." "Why are you so helpless (or annoying or slow or stubborn)?" Thoughts and words carry incredible power to shape and shift your biology and energy. Each time you think or speak a negative phrase, you emit the vibration of that statement and its energetic dust begins to float through the home. The quickest way to stop the impact is to simply say "CANCEL" as soon as you become aware that you're spreading a negative or hurtful message. Instantly, you've stopped the ripple of that vibration. If another person always speaks negatively, consider explaining to them how their words or attitude affects the home. Even if they are not receptive, you can still clear the air by asserting your authority as the care-taker of the home's sacred space. Cancel their negativity by being aware of what's happening, refusing to allow their dust to land on you, and by creating a stronger positive vibration.

- Music – Music is an actual vibration – a subtle yet powerful tool to shift the energy of your home without saying a word. Pandora, Spotify and YouTube have playlists for every mood and musical taste. As the sound waves resonate through the air, every cell in your body begins to align with the "mood" of the song. This is why we choose certain songs when we want to set the stage for a romantic evening and quite a different playlist of songs when we workout. The next time you feel grumpy, experiment with playing cheerful or beautiful music. You'll create a positive vibration that you or your family can literally "tune" to.

- Essential Oils – For centuries, oils have played a vital role in cleansing, purifying, healing and nourishing. Essential oils such as lemon, lavender, peppermint and cinnamon can be used to physically disinfect and cleanse your home. Other oils play a powerful role in caring for your sacred space. Because essential oils have a direct effect on our brains, simply smelling them signals the release of specific hormones and chemicals which can change our state of being. Essential oil companies like DoTerra and Young Living have created oil blends to encourage specific emotional responses. Some of my favorite blends are Forgiveness, Harmony, Hope, Joy, Peace & Calming and Courage. Purchase a simple diffuser to disperse the oil into the air where everyone can breathe it. On more than one occasion, I diffused Joy and watched my teenager's mood change. She complained at first, but she had to breathe! One afternoon, my cat was meowing and moaning restlessly, driving us all crazy. He laid down and purred contentedly within minutes when I dabbed some Peace & Calming on him! Note: some oils are not safe for pets or children, so be sure to research.

- Burning Sage – Although sage is often used in new age or spiritual practices, scientific evidence exists to prove that the release of the scent and particles into the air actually cleanses air-borne bacteria and produces positive energetic results. Sage represents freshening and new beginnings so it is appropriate to use when moving into a new home or to signify the beginning of a new chapter in your life. Some people use sage when doing spring or fall cleaning. It can also be used to clear the air after an argument or a particularly stressful day.

- Himalayan Salt Lamp – Not only do salt lamps provide a comforting glow, they also purify the air and have proven health benefits such as fighting fatigue, increasing productivity and creativity, encouraging better sleep cycles, allergy relief and more!

- Spend Time Outside – One of the best ways to release negative energy dust is to make direct contact with the earth. Grounding (being barefoot on the earth) literally resets the electrical energy of your body. According to Dr. Stephen Sinatra, contact with the earth can "restore and stabilize the bioelectrical circuitry that governs your physiology and organs, harmonize your basic biological rhythms, boost self-healing mechanisms, reduce inflammation and pain, and improve your sleep and feeling of calmness."[4] Inhaling the negative ions found near moving water, like rivers, waterfalls and the beach, stimulates biochemical reactions that increase serotonin, relieve stress, ease depression and boost energy. And of course, exercising, having fun and making memories with others outdoors also shifts your body toward a more positive vibration. Hide and seek, anyone?

- Dust While You Dust – Infuse your common cleaning activities with a deeper purpose. Opening windows, sweeping floors, washing dishes, doing laundry and, of course, dusting are all actions that freshen and cleanse your physical home. As you perform these routine tasks, envision that you are also cleansing the sacred space of your home. You can even speak this out loud, *"I sweep all negative energy out of this room"* as you vacuum or *"As I rinse these dishes, I wash away the stress of this day."* Simply thinking these thoughts alters the vibration in your mind and body. Speaking them out loud is even more powerful.

It's time to verbally dust your home. Remember that energy keeps coming back, just like dust. Verbally dusting is not a "once and done" project, but this simple method takes only a few seconds. Think of it as the equivalent of shaking the dust out of a rug or sweeping fallen leaves off your front step. Use the words below or your own:

"As the care-taker of this space, I consciously and intentionally clear this energy of _____ and I bless my home with _____."

For example: "I consciously and intentionally clear this energy of bickering and I bless my home with connection and fun." or "I clear this energy of sadness and I bless my home with hope and joy."

Do not dismiss this practice as too simple or corny to work. Consistent, daily verbal dusting creates powerful awareness and clears the way for new neural pathways to support healthier thought patterns. In turn, these thoughts will be reflected in different choices and behavior. That's nothing to sneeze at!

Critters

O ur 160-plus-year-old home nestles among tall pines in a remote wilderness region where winter temperatures can reach -120 degrees. Brrrr! All of this breathtaking beauty and proximity to nature means that when the temperature plunges, critters try to sneak into our home for refuge. Over the years, we've had our share of mice, voles, squirrels, a snake (I'm still shuddering!) and the most common intruders – spiders that lurk in the cracks and crevices, creeping out at night and re-spinning their webs in the exact places I just cleaned the day before!

While dust filters into your home and just sits there minding its own business, critters present a more serious problem. Once a critter wriggles into your home, it claims a corner and begins to build a home for itself. In YOUR home. Critters chew on your things, scuttle about in the night, weave stringy, sticky webs and poop wherever they please. They make messes in your home, and while these are *not your messes*, you get stuck cleaning them up anyway.

You can diligently knock down webs, sweep up droppings and barricade your food in containers, but as long as the critter evades detection, you are fighting a losing battle. The only way to stop the mess is to evict the critters!

When it comes to the sacred space of your home, a host of energetic intruders also try to sneak in and set up residence. You can't put your finger on what's wrong, but you feel stressed, irritable, exhausted, drained and angry. Mentally, you tally your blessings - a job, a home, healthy children, food in the fridge, enough money to buy Starbucks, friends who have your back. Yet you can't shake the feeling that life is hard, you can never catch a break and people are jerks.

You feel guilty for struggling when you have so much to be grateful for.

When you find yourself sighing a lot, worrying about other people's issues and constantly cleaning up drama messes that are not your own, you know that you're dealing with a critter problem. You've become tangled in a web spun by another person who has somehow gained entry into the atmosphere of your home!

Critters squeeze in through the tiniest of openings around windows, doors and foundations – cracks and crevices so small that you may not even know they exist. Emotional critters also sneak in through unguarded openings in your life. Places where you're weary, wounded, unaware or perhaps attached to a person or a particular outcome in an unbalanced way.

What are the potential openings in your sacred space?

As you interact with others throughout your day, you experience countless "critter" moments – openings where another person's issues or energy invades your mind and emotions.

- snarky office gossip
- the friend who constantly shares her marriage problems
- the ongoing feud between your sister and your mom
- your grown child's financial struggle
- loud arguments wafting in the window from the neighbors
- the way that other mom corrected your child at the playground
- the ugly custody battle with your ex
- the friend who suddenly seems too busy for you

Before you know it, you're lying awake at 2am, worrying, praying, replaying conversations and feeling weighed down with all of these needs. The critters have found their way in and now they're setting up housekeeping. If you look closely, you'll see emotional webs swinging from your spiritual rafters and little dirty turds in corners of your sacred space.

On a recent afternoon, I heard myself sigh for what seemed like the thousandth time. I stopped and took a moment to tune into my thoughts. To my surprise, every single thing racing through my brain was someone else's life struggle. My own life was just fine that afternoon, but I felt just as heavily burdened as if I were experiencing terrible stress. My precious energy was being drained as I fretted about the decisions that others were making – decisions over which I had zero control. In fact, no one had even asked for my worry or boundless wisdom to be shared!

Because of the intricate link between our minds and bodies, my concern over all of these situations was triggering downloads of stress chemicals and hormones into my body. Not only could this impact my own health and well-being, but it also caused me to send out energetic vibrations of irritation, fear and discouragement. NOT what I want the atmosphere in my home to be!

We care. It's what we do. But caring does not mean that we have to allow the critters of other people's dysfunction to move in and live with us. You have no obligation to allow anyone else's hurt, anger or sadness to saturate the atmosphere that you breathe.

Nowhere in the "good friend contract" does it say that you must be the emotional landlord for your friend's drama.

It's not just other people's issues that creep in. An endless supply of news and opinion streams into your home through your TV, laptop and smartphone. Just a few years ago, people only worried about their immediate family, their hometown and a few nightly news headlines. Now modern technology floods you with stories of tragedy and drama from hometowns all over the world.

I don't even watch the news, and yet it is almost impossible to escape the constant barrage of negativity. As I write these words, our country reels from political tensions, racial injustices, gun violence, heartbreaking stories of sexual abuse, terrorists slamming cars into crowds, the threat of nuclear missile launches, a nation-wide heroin epidemic, skyrocketing Lyme disease, deadly ecoli breakouts from romaine lettuce, brutal hurricanes striking our shores … need I go on?

You probably feel worse just from reading that paragraph. (I'm sorry!)

A smart homeowner seeks out and seals the openings where cold, bugs, noise and unwanted critters can enter. In the same way, it is important to make conscious choices about what you allow into your home's sacred space. Just as fresh air and spiders can enter through the same window, the openings that bring you a wealth of information and entertainment can also allow negativity and stress to enter your home.

Social media is a perfect example of an opening that can allow both positive and negative to enter your home. We wake up in a pretty good mood, roll over and pick up our phones. After 5-10 minutes of scrolling through the latest news feeds, our brains are filled with everything from Aunt Sally's meatloaf recipe to our friend's latest political rant to a fundraiser for a friend-of-a-friend-of-a-friend's child battling cancer. Before we crawl out of bed, we are already emotionally overloaded and there are not enough cute puppy videos out there to undo the damage.

Living in a bubble is not the answer. We need healthy connections and that includes interacting with friends and family, staying informed of current affairs and even knowing what Aunt Sally had for dinner last night. But we must also be aware and wise. Especially when we are already tired, stressed or sad, emotional critters can squirm more easily through the openings in our tender hearts and create messes in our minds and emotions.

Over time, the critters grow and reproduce until their droppings and webs fill your mind and influence the way you live. You find yourself angry or sad or offended on behalf of other people – many of whom you'll never meet. The whole world seems wrong and life feels heavy – even when things are going well in your personal life!

Creating a safe and healing space includes screening what and who has access to your precious home.

My brother is an exterminator by trade. Daily, he faces critter infestations that would give the rest of us nightmares for weeks. He knows all the tricks to locating the offending culprits, ushering them out and closing up the holes. Each time my brother completes a job, he feels the satisfaction of giving the home-owner peace of mind. Trust me, he doesn't lose a moment's sleep feeling badly for the roaches or rodents who've been removed.

You would not allow your family to live in a rodent, spider-infested physical home and neither should you allow the sacred space of your home to become filthy with the messes of outside influences. Don't feel guilty if you need to close your home to certain people or influences. After all, it's your home – not theirs. You can be an informed citizen and "be there" for your friends and family while still consciously guarding your peace of mind. Nothing that brings emotional harm or stress into your home should be given a warm welcome!

Here are some of the common ways that emotional critters can enter your home:

- News reports
- Songs with themes of hard luck, substance abuse, unhealthy relationships, cheating, breakups, revenge on exes, etc. (most of the popular music these days!)
- TV shows featuring storylines of violence, terror or emotional trauma like sexual abuse, serial killers, stressful situations that trigger fight or flight responses in the viewer
- Video games that focus on violence and stress/fear situations
- Humor that degrades others or reality shows that exploit the participants' drama or misery (we love these shows but they strengthen the vibrations of drama in our own lives)
- Social media can be a source of venting, arguing and oversharing the drama in other people's lives
- Working or living with a negative person
- Allowing a friend or partner to gripe constantly to you
- Spending more time with friends who drain you vs. friends who fill you
- Venting or gossiping about acquaintances, relatives or co-workers

The following suggestions are simple. I'm sure you've seen or heard them from multiple other sources, but perhaps you've not considered them in light of creating a home that is a sanctuary. More than just good suggestions, they are essential critter management. Just because you can't see the emotional rats scurrying across the room doesn't mean they aren't affecting your quality of life. Your precious time and energy drain away when you allow the issues and dramas of others to occupy your thoughts. Eventually, the stress affects your health and spreads to others around you. It's time to take back your space!

CRITTER CONTROL

- When you feel stressed or upset, ask yourself, "Is anything actually wrong in MY life at this very moment?" Often, you'll realize that things are ok! Then it's time to consider the possibility that you're tapping into another person's issue or energy.

- Declare news/phone/TV free zones or times of day. Especially guard the first moments of your morning. Try to begin your day with something positive or beautiful. A few moments on your porch breathing in the fresh air is way better than a dose of Instagram. Many families implement a no-phones-at-the-table policy. At the end of the day, experts recommend not looking at a screen for at least an hour before bed. Keeping electronics out of your bedroom lowers your exposure to EMF radiation as well as prevents you from ending your day with yet another dose of bad news, drama or the discouragement of comparing your life with the carefully curated lives of others.

- Purposely share GOOD news. Collect fun video clips, stories or happy songs to share with your partner or children. Laughter releases much-needed endorphins into your body, so find a funny show that you can enjoy regularly. Intentionally notice beauty and let it soak into your soul. Pointing out, "Look at that sunset!" will lift everyone's vibration.

- Spend the majority of your social time with positive, loving people. This can be hard to do if you live or work closely with a negative person! If you can't avoid time with them, try to shift the conversations to more positive topics. Limit the gossip, whining and general complaining that has become so culturally accepted that it's almost expected. Rise above and elevate others with you!

- Do a social media fast. Even an hour makes a difference. Through the constant flow of your news feeds, dozens of others energetically stroll through your sacred space. By stepping away from your phone or laptop, you are booting them out so that you can enjoy your home in peace for a few hours. Rather than focusing on the world "out there," consciously engage in the world around you. Pay attention to yourself. What do you need? Notice beauty. Eat something delicious. Read a book. Talk to your friend. Take a walk. Sleep.

- When you find yourself consumed with a loved one's life decisions or opinions, consciously STOP. Imagine that this person is a spider! No kidding ... this works. Mentally pick them up, carry them outside and lovingly sit them down on the sidewalk. Speak a blessing to them. (You'll learn more about this in the next section of the book.) Now in your imagination, walk back inside and shut the door. Keep your home as drama-free as possible and don't feel guilty about it.

- Be aware that you may be biologically and emotionally addicted to drama and stress. If you feel a little bored when things are calm, you may feel the urge to connect to some stress to stimulate a download of cortisol. Needing to be needed can also drive us to associate with people who demand our attention and assistance. We receive tremendous mental and emotional boosts when we help others. If we aren't careful, we seek that feeling at the expense of our own well-being.

- Remember that we are all homesick for our true home. Most of the negativity, complaining, protesting and venting is really a cry for something deeper. People are worried about the condition of our world. They feel overwhelmed and burdened by the injustices they see. Something within them knows that life should be different, but they don't know how to change it. As you respond with compassion and create a safe space for your own spirit, you will also model for others how to find the peace of home.

- Consciously send Blessing toward each person who impacts your mind and emotions. Speak that they will be safe, loved, happy and wise. When you see a troubling headline, use that as an opportunity to bless those affected by the situation.

Cleansing of Emotional Critters:

"I am grateful that my eyes have been opened to see how I have picked up burdens that are not mine to carry. In so doing, I am allowing the life stresses of others to enter my home, affect my state of mind and impact my emotional health. I forgive myself for not being more vigilant to protect my home. Because I desire my home to be a safe haven, I choose now to make better choices about what influences I allow into my sacred space. I ask for wisdom. Please show me now what situations are weighing me down."

Once a situation comes to your mind, continue...

"I recognize that _____(situation) is impacting my life and my peace. I choose to bless _____ (person) with love, compassion, wisdom and strength. May he/she face these challenges with courage and make life-affirming, healing choices as needed. I am available to help as I am divinely guided to do so. I release myself from needing to carry the weight of this person's choices or life situation. With love, I now cleanse my heart and home of the negative energy from _____. I rest in knowing that all things are working for their best and highest good – no matter how circumstances look on the surface. I bless my home with deep peace and lightness of spirit. All is well and all shall be well."

You live in a hurting world. If you are a sensitive or empathetic person, it is impossible to avoid feeling the pain of others. While you possess special gifts that are needed in this world, remember that lying awake at night worrying about situations over which you have no control is NOT your calling. I recommend saying the above prayer every evening or whenever you feel the pressure and stress of another person's life impacting yours.

Clutter

Mention the word "clutter" and you'll hear a collective groan. Most of us fight a constant battle against never-ending piles of dishes, laundry, school papers, toys, socks, pet hair, unsorted mail, and more. Flat surfaces in my home sprout piles that mysteriously multiply in the dark. (That's my story and I'm sticking to it!)

Extreme clutter can become a serious and even life-threatening situation. We've all heard the stories of hoarders crushed to death by toppling stacks of their belongings. But for most of us, clutter represents a harmless, unsightly annoyance. We may wish longingly for magazine perfect counters and neat closets, but the truth is that we co-exist quite comfortably with our clutter. We even excuse it away with cute signs that read, "A cluttered desk is a sign of genius" or "Excuse the mess – We're making memories."

Another clutter quote states "Clutter is postponed decisions." I propose that clutter actually IS a decision – the decision to do what is easier at the current moment. We choose to drop clothes on the floor instead of in the hamper, to toss mail on the counter to be sorted later, to go to bed with a sink full of dirty dishes and to put off routine chores until our home requires what my mother called a major "dung out."

As we make these seemingly harmless decisions day after day, they become habits.

Dust and critters enter our homes without permission, but clutter is all our doing! For some reason, we choose the immediate satisfaction instead of the longer-term gain. Over time, our clutter stops being innocent and becomes symbolic of a deeply ingrained pattern of behavior. We've reached the point that we need an entire weekend of cleaning and organizing just to find our garage floor. No matter how often we promise ourselves we will change our ways, the clutter returns.

Physical clutter often masks deeper emotional issues. One young woman I know has struggled her entire life to keep her spaces clean. From her childhood bedroom to her college dorm. From her first apartment to a lovely three-bedroom home. No matter how often she vowed to be neat and tidy, she still found herself surrounded by a furious jumble of dirty clothes, dishes crusted with old food, empty soda cans and crumpled candy wrappers.

When you know this young woman's story, her struggle makes more sense. Her earliest years were spent shuttling between multiple foster homes. With each move, she learned that the people and things she loved could be torn away at a moment's notice – that she should not attach to anything that could be temporary. Because each of her living spaces did not feel like a permanent home, she could not and would not allow herself to show them love by cleaning, organizing or decorating. In effect, the hundreds of unconscious, cluttering choices she made each day kept the little child inside trapped in the emotions of feeling homeless, unwanted and unworthy.

Once she became aware of what her clutter represented, she could choose to make different decisions. Slowly, she began clearing her clutter one box at a time. Putting up a Christmas tree represented a big step toward understanding that she can create a home anywhere - even in a temporary space. She is beginning to believe that she deserves a blessed home where she can flourish.

Your sacred space also becomes cluttered one small decision at a time. Once again, you make the decision to postpone cleaning up your sacred space. It is easier to hold a grudge, to stay up too late night after night, to complain and nag, to handle stress with a swig of alcohol or a shopping spree. It's easy to justify these little momentary choices. After all, it was a #*%(#%^ day and you deserve to relax and let off a little steam. You're aware that you're not really dealing with things, but you promise that you'll tidy up that emotional clutter another day soon.

As the emotional clutter grows in your mind and heart, each decision strengthens and fuels the very emotional energies you don't want. Depression. Anger. Fear. Grief. Strong, resonating energies are set in motion. Unless something stops the ripples, they will spread, tuning even more energy toward that negative emotion. The clutter continues to grow.

Emotions are sent to deliver a message and pass on through.

They are not intended to be lifelong soulmates.

Your body is designed to handle emotions and clear them when their work is finished. Just like sorting and tossing junk mail! When you don't release a strong emotion, it piles on top of the last uncleared emotion. Like clutter spreading from table to floor to hallway, these dominant emotions begin to affect the atmosphere of your home.

Remember the tuning forks? As a negative vibration strengthens, others around you begin to resonate with that dominant emotion too. Over time, it can feel almost impossible to change the pattern. You can see this effect in families where everyone has a hot temper. Or in another home where multiple family members battle depression, anxiety or chronic complaining. Your home can get caught in an energetic "whirlpool" that keeps everyone spinning deeper and deeper into the strongest emotions.

When left uncleared, your dominant emotions create spiritual clutter that is just as real as piles of mail, laundry and scum in the tub. One day you look around and say, "MY LIFE IS A MESS!" as you realize that your life bears little resemblance to the life you dreamed of.

Signs of emotional clutter:

- Feeling stuck - no matter what you do, you can't seem to break out of a certain behavior or circumstance
- Repeating patterns in your life – you repeat the same unhealthy choices for your body, finances, relationships, etc.
- Re-occurring thoughts – like a broken record playing over and over in your mind
- Hearing yourself say the same negative phrases a lot
- Feeling controlled by a consistent strong emotion like anger, depression or fear – it has become part of your identity
- Rehashing the same arguments with others (or with yourself!)

Just as with physical clutter, attempting to do a major cleanup of your mind and emotions does no good unless you change the habit that created the clutter. Breaking the pattern of clutter doesn't happen overnight. You have to create new habits one decision at a time – picking up your emotional socks, rinsing your spiritual dishes, choosing to use kinder words, doing the work to heal your heart. The first step is recognizing that you have a clutter problem and deciding that you truly want to live differently.

The problem is that we have a love/hate relationship with our clutter. As much as I complain about the piles on my desk, the truth is that I just don't feel right working at a shiny, clean desk. Every time I clear my desk, I quickly revert to the habits that create the paper piles because they feel familiar and safe.

Emotional clutter can be comforting as well. When you've lived in a dominant energy of sadness for years, happiness may actually feel weird to you. Someone who lives in the constant vibration that life is unfair will often feel oddly empty or suspicious when something goes in their favor. If your body chemistry has been conditioned to expect high stress and drama, you may purposely pick a fight or start drama when things get too calm. Your body needs its "fix" of familiar chemicals.

On the other end of the spectrum, you may feel claustrophobic or agitated when surrounded by clutter. Some people feel compelled to create extreme order in their outer world to counteract intense inner turmoil. One of my good friends often responds to tension with a deep cleaning spree, scrubbing every surface and tossing toys and clothes until she can "breathe again."

Once you identify the dominant energies and emotional habits in your home, you can take steps to change them. Like decluttering your physical home, progress may seem slow. It takes time to reprogram your brain and to reset the chemical/hormonal code of your body.

Since childhood, my emotional set point has been sadness and grief. Once I recognized this, I could make intentional choices to heal and reverse my body's dependency on these emotions. I felt empowered, but it still took months for me to feel comfortable with positive emotions like joy or fun or hope. My instinct was still to sink into sadness rather than to consciously cultivate joy.

Little by little, you can break the hold of even major emotions like anger and depression. As you create new emotional patterns and habits, your body and spirit will begin to shift. You will create new neural pathways that will rewire your brain. Your relationships will change as well because your energy will be lighter and freer. This is the power of cleansing and blessing at work. Every small step forward increases your courage and freedom to make even more healing choices for your home.

Clearing the Clutter

- Identify Your Dominant Emotions – How do you feel most days? Where are things "piling up" emotionally? Can you spot emotional patterns in yourself? Are certain times of the day harder? Certain topics? What emotions are so entrenched

59

that they feel almost like part of your personality? What do you excuse by saying "That's just who I am?" What do you see happening in your children? Do you feel attached to the familiarity of your emotions – even though you say you hate feeling this way? Do you fear that letting go of your dominant emotions would change you too much?

- Honor the Emotions – Try not to label emotions as good or bad. While some emotions are clearly more enjoyable, all emotions are important messengers. Like the Check Engine light in your car, they alert you to what is happening under the hood of your life. Often, your inner world just wants to be heard! *Hey … you're really stressed. You need to pay attention to this red flashing STRESS light and rearrange your schedule instead of yelling at the kids!* Whether positive or negative, listen to the emotion. It may be your response to an imperfection you see in the world. Perhaps your distress is really an inner cry for home. Thank the emotion for showing you where your life needs extra love and blessing.

- Let Unwanted Emotions Leave – Think of negative emotions as UPS drivers delivering a package to your porch. Receive what they are delivering and then let them drive away. Just because a strong emotion of loneliness shows up at your door on a quiet Tuesday afternoon doesn't mean you have to invite it in for tea, offer it a bedroom or add its name to your family tree. Allowing the emotion to deliver its message and leave is profoundly healing. On the other hand, holding onto an emotion keeps the vibration going. We tend to collect familiar emotions that match the inner messages we already hold. Over time, these patterns grow so strong and deep that the emotions begin to feel like part of you. The good news is that we can use this knowledge to weaken the grip of emotions we don't enjoy and to create positive emotional patterns as well. Who wouldn't like to have a deeply ingrained pattern of joy?

After you've taken some time to really listen to the emotion and understand what message it is bringing to you, use the following as an example for honoring and releasing an emotion: *"Thank you,_____. (name of emotion) I hear you. Thank you for bringing an important message about _____ to me so that I can change the things that I can change. Thank you for helping me to care for my spirit and to create an even more beautiful life. Now you are free to go. I lovingly release you and bless my home with _____ (the opposite emotion).*

- Break the Power of Old Habits - Childhood trauma, fear or abuse creates re-occurring emotional reactions that tangibly change the brain patterns and biology of your body. The trapped emotions from early experiences shape the way you see the world and form lifelong emotional coping skills such as manipulation, controlling others through anger, never letting anyone get close to you, withdrawing from conflict, stress eating, etc. Breaking these life-long habits will require more intentional methods of healing and releasing the underlying emotion. Therapy can be a useful tool, but if the thought of talking about your issues makes your hair curl, you'll be happy to know that there are some excellent resources available to help clear stuck or trapped emotions. My favorites are *The Emotion Code, The Emotional Freedom Technique* and *The Tapping Solution* (See Resources at the end of the book) which teach simple do-it-yourself techniques to clear emotions.

- Replace the Habit – Once you've cleared emotional clutter, you're ready to make new, positive decisions. Remember that you'll need to decide to do what's BEST rather than what's easiest. Choose one small new emotional habit at a time such as beginning your day with a moment of gratitude or taking a 15-minute walk at lunch. Maybe you'll decide to open a difficult conversation you've been avoiding. Or you'll end your day with a restorative soak in the tub rather than a mindless scroll through social media. When you feel yourself escalating into a familiar emotional response of anger or anxiety or sadness, stop the ripple and make a different decision. You may have to talk yourself down by saying out loud "I am not going to live like this anymore. I choose _____." Just as a million little harmless decisions led to the mess, each small healing decision moves you toward the life you want. Make the decision to notice beauty, to embrace humor, to nourish yourself with spectacular food, to speak kindly to yourself and others. With each small decision, visualize that you are washing your insides with new, healing chemicals and hormones and resetting your body to a more loving and peaceful state ... because you are!

- Ask for Help – If you are not able to handle or heal your emotions from painful experiences like abuse, betrayal or chronic depression, do not hesitate to seek help through counseling or prayer ministries. Far from being weak or selfish, pursuing inner healing is one of the most loving things you can do for yourself and your loved ones. I experienced a huge turning point when I decided that I did not want to leave a legacy of sadness to my children. They deserved a joyful mother and I realized that my healing would give them hope to pursue their own. When you clear your home of negative dominant emotions, others will feel safer and more cherished in your presence. By refusing to deal with your issues, you end up hurting those you love and modeling for them that they, too, should not ask for help.

- Make Amends -- Even though you do your best to hide your struggles, strong emotions affect others. Perhaps you carry such a weight of sadness that you have no energy to play with your child. Depression can keep you detached and distant from your loved ones for days or weeks. Harsh words, spoken from your own pain and frustration, can frighten or crush your child's spirit. Left unchecked, strong dominant emotions continue to expand and create generations of unhealthy homes. Someone has to break the cycle. Apologize to those you've hurt intentionally or unintentionally by your words and actions. Take responsibility for your own emotional sacred space. Even if others choose to stay trapped in their dominant emotions, you can shift the atmosphere by cleansing your own emotions and bringing Blessing into the home.

- Teach Your Children to Release Emotions – Emotional habits form at an early age. Already, your child has developed ways of coping and reacting to life. As he responds to the dominant emotions within and around him, he is growing accustomed to the familiar chemical downloads triggered by the environment of your home. When your child has a strong emotion, use it as a teachable moment. Show him how to express it safely, understand it, thank it and then let it go in favor of a more positive emotion. The ability to return from a fearful, sad or angry state to a state of joy is a significant stage in a child's brain development. Each time your child returns to joy, they strengthen the appropriate brain synapses, allowing them to return more quickly the next time. At first, they will need you to help them know that all is well when they skin their knee or break a toy or fail a test. As they mature, they will learn to bring themselves back to joy. Teach them that emotions are temporary messengers and that good moments will return. (NOTE: Every time YOU return to joy, you are also building your own trust and healing your mind and body!)

- Embrace the Process – Through Blessing, you can trade stress for peace. Anger for understanding. Depression for hope. But it will take time. You can't switch things up for a day or two and declare that it "didn't work for me." When you start a new vibration, it's a baby one. If you've been reverberating with rage for a long time, it takes time to grow an equally powerful calm vibration. But you can begin anew at any moment. Hundreds of times a day if needed!

- End the Day With Release – Clutter experts tell us that small, consistent daily changes are the key to conquering the mountains of chaos. One of my favorite organizing pros is the Flylady. Her claim to fame is her practice of "shining your sink" every evening.[5] She knows that over time, creating this one spot of order each day will empower you to clear another spot and another. Shine your spiritual sink each evening by honoring and releasing any strong emotions that have been part of that day. Did you exchange angry words with someone? Are you feeling frustrated with your career? Are you struggling with loneliness? Some of the wisest advice ever given is: "Do not let the sun go down while you are still angry."[6] We can easily expand that to include not letting the sun go down while we are still anxious, insecure, fearful, sad or holding onto any other emotion that has been part of our day. As much as possible, try to go to sleep each night with a clean emotional slate. Long-held pain or deep beliefs will take longer to clear, but by doing some emotional house-keeping each night, you can keep spiritual clutter from building up. Each healthy decision is like removing another piece of junk mail from the pile. Eventually, you can see the clear counter space!

Nightly Release Prayer:

"I come to the end of this day with a grateful heart. No matter what has happened today, I choose to receive it as working for my highest good. I honor every emotion that came to the surface today. I hear you. Now as I prepare to rest, I choose to release the stress, fear, anger, arguments, shame, sadness, loneliness … all of it. I choose to trust that

all situations will be resolved in a clear, simple and loving manner. I choose to forgive _____ *for* _____ *even though I may not understand their behavior or even believe they deserve forgiveness. I choose to exchange my dominant emotion of* _____ *for a blessing of* _____ *(opposite emotion). None of this is possible in my own strength, so I ask for Divine courage and wisdom that I may continue to cleanse and heal tomorrow. For now, I settle into the deep rest of knowing that all is well. My home is a sanctuary where I can rest, connect and flourish. I open my heart to receive all of the blessings that are headed my way. I embrace the peace, joy and love that is my truest design and destiny. Thank you and may it be so."*

Cosmetic

We sure do love a good home improvement show. Night after night, millions of us curl up on our couches to watch our favorite handymen and women demolish and design, fix and flip. As dilapidated, down-right ugly houses transform into magazine-worthy beauties, our inner fixer-upper comes to life. We catch a glimpse of the possibility that meaning and beauty can also be reclaimed from the rubble of our lives.

Home improvement shows give us hope that no matter what design or décor nightmares have occurred in a home's past, they can be FIXED! Don't like that wall between the kitchen and dining room? Knock it down! Hate the pink tile in the bathroom? No problem! Backyard a tangle of overgrown weeds? An afternoon with a chainsaw can tame the jungle! By the end of each episode, we feel inspired and empowered. Whether or not we ever pick up a hammer or paintbrush, we love to know that we could if we wanted to badly enough.

When a family moves out of a house, they leave behind the physical evidence of their life - stains on a rug, a crayon mark on a wall, the odd-colored formica countertop, the porch they added ten years ago. One of the first things the new home-owner does is make a list of things to repair, replace or renovate.

We can easily see the physical changes we want to make, but it's a little harder to recognize a home's spiritual and emotional history. What was life really like behind closed doors? What was the dominant energy of their home? What evidence remains in the sacred space long after they've left?

We often look around an older home and say, "If only these walls could talk." The truth is that they do! A home becomes a museum, documenting both the physical and spiritual history of those who've lived there. When you understand the way spiritual energy works, some things may begin to make sense.

Have you experienced any of these things since moving into your current home?

- Your children have been bickering more than usual
- You or your spouse seem irritable for no apparent reason
- You aren't sleeping well or have bad dreams
- You feel anxiety, depression or another emotion that you didn't experience before
- Your family gets sick more often
- You feel angrier or sadder in certain rooms or at certain times of the day

All of these and more can be a signs of residual or leftover energy in your home. You may be tuning into emotional ripples set in motion by the dominant vibrations of past residents. Remember earlier in the book when I said that none of us would move in and live in the middle of the former owner's discarded garbage? Unknowingly, we live surrounded by spiritual remains all the time.

The older the home, the more layers of history are stored in its sacred space.

Our move to New York was nothing short of miraculous.. I loved my new home and couldn't wait to build a new life in our small mountain town. Shortly after moving, I began to battle deep loneliness and sadness. I was caught off guard and shocked by the intensity of these emotions. At times, the heaviness felt unbearable – especially on quiet days when I worked alone in the kitchen.

After almost a year of living in our home, I learned some fascinating information about one of the former owners. Once a guide leading expeditions in the Adirondack mountains, he suffered a stroke in his 40's that left him confined to his bed for almost two decades. His family set up a small bed for him in the mudroom just off the kitchen so that he could be nearby. Year after year, he laid there feeling helpless, frustrated and claustrophobic (it's a very tiny room). I'm sure he deeply grieved the active life he had lost and no doubt felt lonely when his family was out and about. These strong, persistent emotions created an energy that remained in the kitchen area of the home long after he passed.

I believe that much of the grief and loneliness I felt in the kitchen was the result of my spirit tuning into the strong energy left behind in that space. An energy that would continue to resonate until it was countered by a stronger vibration. I began to play cheerful music and talk to friends on the telephone while cooking as a way to reverse the vibration of being alone and sad.

Our family experienced another marked change after moving into our home. We began to have heated arguments. Even in little matters, we felt a strong need to express ourselves and a determination to win at all costs. No one would back down! This was unusual behavior for us – especially for my husband and I who had never been angry or argumentative people. Needless to say, this did not contribute to an atmosphere of peace and joy.

Then we began to learn more about the woman who had lived in the house for over 60 years. People around town described her as a strong, forceful woman who spoke her mind and always got her way. We learned that this woman single-handedly convinced the state of New York to alter the plans for their proposed highway, creating a sweeping curve around her (our) house! While we certainly had our share of strong personalities coupled with teenage attitude, our family was also tuning to the residual energy of her strong will when we were upset.

Once we recognized the effects of our home's past history, we made conscious choices to clear that trapped energy and create more positive vibrations. We had already removed the former owner's discarded furniture and faded curtains. Now we also had the choice to clear out leftover depression, anxiety and argumentativeness. As we filled the atmosphere with intentional blessings, we experienced a greater level of harmony and fun in our home.

Thankfully, past history isn't always negative! Whatever happens in your home leaves its energy for those who follow. When you love deeply, you leave behind love. When you fill your home with affection and joy, it resonates with a beautiful energy. The home of a creative, resourceful and courageous person will inspire the next occupant. If you find yourself singing more, enjoying a new interest in gardening or feeling passionate about making a difference in your community, you may be walking in the footsteps of your home's former owners.

> **Actively cleansing and blessing your sacred space benefits not only your own life, but also leaves a wonderful legacy for the next occupants of your home.**

You need not fear the history or memories within the walls of your home any more than you fear the color of the paint on those walls. As the spiritual caretaker of your home, you have the right to demolish, design, renovate and fix up anything that has been left behind. Making the sacred space of your home YOURS is one of the most powerful ways to feel "at home."

- Notice any unusual new behaviors – Are you struggling in ways you haven't before? Do you feel more restless or angry or depressed? Do your pets or children seem agitated?
- Research your home's history – If you live in an older home, check your town library archives for any history preserved there. Talk to your neighbors to learn about the former

residents. Listen for clues like "she got the house in the divorce" or "their daughter died of cancer" or "he would lend a helping hand anytime you needed" or "we never saw them outside" or "we really miss them." Each of these can give you insight into what vibrations may have been dominant in your home.

- Change what you don't like - Even if you can't determine specific historical issues, you can still decide the kind of home you want to live in. Routinely cleanse and care for your sacred space. Rewrite your home's history by filling the atmosphere with good memories, beauty, nourishing foods, kind words and blessings!

- If you identify a specific dominant energy that has been left behind, use the following to clear it:

"I honor the history of this home and all those who have lived here – experiencing both good times and hard times. As the new resident of this space, I desire to create my own memories and to establish this home as a safe and loving place. I recognize that the strong energy of _____ (negative emotion) is part of the history of this home. This energy is not part of my story and so I respectfully cleanse it through my God-given authority as the spiritual owner of this space. May every room in this house where _____ (negative emotion) has resonated now be filled with _____. (the opposite blessing) I accept my role in caring for this home and writing the next chapter of its history. It is my heartfelt intention to leave behind a legacy of peace, healing and love."

Company

The darkness of the bedroom slowly faded to gray as I burrowed deeper under my covers. About 20 minutes earlier, my husband's truck had roared to life, the tires crunching over the snowy driveway as he left for work. This unofficial alarm clock signaled that it was almost time to roll out of bed and start my day.

Stretching and shivering in anticipation of the morning chill, I was surprised to hear the mudroom door slam. Its rattly latch made an unmistakable clunk that sounded different from any other door in our home. Heavy boots stomped off snow and then the door to the kitchen opened.

Wayne must have come back home to get something he forgot, I thought, picking up my phone to check the weather forecast for the day. Now I heard him moving about the kitchen, clanking dishes and running water. *He's going to be so late for work!*

"Why did you come back home?" I texted his phone, still not ready to exit the warm bed.

A few seconds later his reply arrived, "I just pulled into the job site."

"Wait …. you're not downstairs?"

"Nope. I'm a hard-working man. Not all of us can sleep in, you know …."

Now I was definitely awake! Sitting up in bed, I listened to the continuing movements below me. The water stopped running and the dishwasher door closed with a thump.

Stepping from the warm safety of my blankets, I pulled on my bathrobe, pattered down the stairs and peered around the corner into the kitchen. Just as I expected, the room was completely empty.

Had I seen a man standing in my kitchen, I would have fled back up the stairs, trembling as I dialed 911. Instead, I merely shook my

71

head and poured myself a glass of water to start the day. It was not the first time that I had experienced the sounds of unseen visitors in our home.

Home should be our safe place. Behind our walls and doors, we expect privacy and protection from the outside world. When an intruder crosses these boundaries, we feel violated and rightfully so. Climbing through people's windows or breaking through locked doors can get you locked up!

But what about unseen visitors? Especially in an older home, you may suddenly sense that you are not alone. No one else is in the room, but you experience a sensation, an unexplained shiver, the waft of a scent, the swish of air moving as if someone is passing by. In some cases, you may actually see an object move or hear voices, running water or doors opening and closing.

Before you throw the book and run screaming, let me assure you that these incidents are far more common than you may realize. Many people experience mysterious encounters but never tell anyone. Sometimes we don't even admit them to ourselves because we feel uncomfortable with what we can't explain or understand.

In many parts of the world, what we consider extraordinary occurrences are simply part of everyday life. These cultures accept the reality of an unseen realm and live with greater awareness, a blurring of the lines between physical and spiritual worlds. Our Western mindset has been programmed to accept only what can be explained and experienced, analyzed and categorized.

We easily believe in the physical world because we experience it in tangible ways. We taste the familiar bite of our morning coffee, smell its invigorating aroma, feel the warmth as we wrap our hands around our favorite mug and hear the clank as we sit the mug on the hard surface of a nearby table. A table that provides a visible, touchable, completely logical place to sit a coffee mug.

The physical world makes so much sense that we often assume that it is the only world that exists.

While I am certainly no paranormal expert, I've had enough experiences to realize that our world overlaps with another, teeming with a life of its own. Lest you think the unseen world is a new age or pagan idea, even the Bible teaches that we live surrounded by a "great cloud of witnesses"[7] which scholars believe to be saints who have lived, died and now dwell in a heavenly realm. Although gone from this physical world, they are still able to witness our lives and cheer us on.

The physical and spiritual realms are so intricately linked that many scientists now believe that time and space, as we understand them, do not actually exist. We've devised a linear calendar to organize what we know as chronological time. We follow maps that define the boundaries of cities, states, countries and continents. Making sense of where we are in time and space helps us to feel more secure. First responders at an accident scene often ask orienting questions about today's date, home address and the current US President in order to determine if a crash victim has a grasp on reality.

But is the reality we grasp so firmly a comfortable, narrow reality of our own creation? Scientists working in the field of quantum physics propose that there are actually many layers of time and civilization co-existing simultaneously. Let that sink in for a moment. If this is true, then you may actually be a "ghost" in someone else's home! (Kinda makes you want to go bang a door or two, doesn't it?)

Most of us go about our day with little to no awareness of the spiritual life taking place around us. We can ignore it so easily because it is usually undetectable by our five senses. But occasionally, often in times of stress or transition, we undeniably encounter another realm. Some people possess a greater sensitivity and intuition that

73

connects them to the spiritual world. One of my friends often sees angels standing in the room with us. A young mother hurried to the nursery to soothe her crying baby only to hear his cry turn to a giggle. Entering the room, she smelled the familiar scent of her grandfather's cologne. Grandpa had died several months earlier. Another acquaintance receives premonitions or an inner message about events that haven't happened yet.

Children also seem more aware of activity in your unseen sacred space. Perhaps because they are still so "new" to this world that they have not fully forgotten the spiritual realm. You may see a child staring, giggling or babbling at what appears to be nothing. Pets can also be sensitive to unseen presences. Your dog may suddenly bark at "nothing" or your cat may seem to chase an invisible object.

If we believe that the physical world is the only reality, then these things seem strange and phenomenal. However, if we view the entire universe as composed of body and spirit, these events simply become natural manifestations of a reality beyond our physical realm.

Paranormal experts tell us that spirits or energies become more active when there is a change or disruption in a space such as a new owner, a major renovation or a new baby. At one of my jobs, I was warned that a mischievous entity loved to prank new employees by jamming the copier and refusing to allow the coffeepot to brew coffee. Sure enough. For the first few weeks, I had to ask someone else to push the copier and coffeepot buttons for me.

A very practical woman (not at all inclined to other-worldly imaginings) shared with me that she walked into her new workplace carrying a mug of coffee. Just as she entered the building, someone shoved her so hard that the mug flew from her hand and shattered on the floor. No one else was nearby except the startled receptionist sitting at a desk across the lobby.

After moving into our home, we experienced several startling incidents and wondered if we'd made a huge mistake. We knew enough by this point to stay calm and seek insight. Before long, we became convinced that the presence we sensed and heard was our home's former owner. After almost a decade of vacancy, his home had been taken over by our lively family banging about, painting, rearranging rooms and living life out loud!

This man's spirit was clearly disturbed by our arrival. So now what? We had no clue how these things worked, weren't even sure we believed in such things and certainly couldn't ask around town, "Hey – any ideas how to appease an angry former owner's spirit?"

Being a reasonable guy, my husband figured that a solid approach would be to discuss the situation man-to-man. He waited until no one else was home and then spoke kindly into the sacred space, introducing himself as the new owner. He shared how much we loved this grand old home and appreciated all of the hard work the previous owners had invested to make it so beautiful. He assured whoever was listening that we would respect the home, restore it and allow others to enjoy it by opening a bed and breakfast. Amazingly, the spirit seemed satisfied and the incidents stopped.

As you intentionally occupy the sacred space you have been entrusted to care for, the spiritual world accepts your ownership and aligns with that reality.

Most of the time, hearing or even seeing spiritual activity is quite harmless with no need to directly interact with or try to remove a spirit or presence in your home. By taking ownership of the sacred space of your home, most opposition or confusion will clear on its own. (If you skipped the chapter titled "Moving In," go back and read it for more on this topic)

Live in a respectful way that honors the past history of the home. Don't make disparaging remarks about former owners, their lousy construction skills or the fuschia paint they chose for the guest room. Refrain from joking about ghosts or trying to chase them off. Don't try to catch them in the act, by setting up cameras or traps. (Trust me, they do not like this!) Avoid setting up any power struggles by asserting yourself unnecessarily. In other words, don't stomp through the house yelling "Hey ... all of you spirits clear out. This is MY house now!"

Over the years, I've come to peace with whatever unseen residents may share my home. I imagine that I'm living in a cosmic apartment building where it is normal to occasionally hear sounds of life from the other tenants. As long as they don't interfere with my own life, I don't worry. By calmly and respectfully carrying on with your life and establishing yourself as the care-taker for your spiritual space, you can also coexist peacefully.

Again, it is best to not intentionally engage an unseen presence unless it is directly interfering with your life. If you sense that a spirit is angry, playing unnecessary tricks or upsetting your children, then use the following to bring some peace.

"Hello ... my name is _____ and I am the new owner (renter, resident, etc) of this home. I understand that you may be upset or concerned about my presence here. I assure you that I do not intend any harm to you or to this home. In fact, I am planning to take excellent care of it. I'm not sure how things work in your world or how much you know about my world. In my world, I have the legal right to live in this home and to create a safe and loving space for myself (and my family). When you _____ (whatever action has been upsetting), it causes _____ in my world. I will do my best to not interfere with your life/world and I respectfully ask you to do the same so that we can all live in peace."

Again ... do not be freaked out by this. It's ok if you don't understand or even believe it. I just want you to know that you are NOT alone. You would be amazed at how many of your friends and family have similar stories to tell! Because our society distances itself from events beyond the visible and observable universe, we choose to keep quiet about supernatural encounters. We don't want others to label us as crazy or our homes as haunted. Understanding the connection between physical and spiritual worlds can demystify these encounters. They are simply signs of the mingling of the visible and invisible, body and spirit of our incredible universe.

Crisis

A ny responsible homeowner can care for dust, critters, clutter, cosmetic changes and company without too much concern. These are all a normal part of living in a home. But when we discover broken water pipes, a sinking foundation, lead paint or serious mold, most of us enlist the help of an expert. These crises fall beyond what we feel comfortable tackling alone.

Your home's sacred space can also contain more serious issues. If you've worked through all of the preceding cleansing methods and you're still experiencing issues, you may be living in a home with a deeply troubled atmosphere.

Some signs of deeper crisis are:

- extremely strong emotion that will not lift (depression, fear or fury)
- feeling unexplained terror - your children seem afraid of things you can't see
- sensing an evil or confrontational presence that feels threatening
- persistent frightening or violent nightmares
- items in your home mysteriously breaking or not working
- odd or unexplained illness
- physical attack by an unseen entity (feeling choked, held down or blocked from entering a room)

These indicators may point to a history of great distress, abuse or even occult practices that have resulted in a spiritual darkness or evil energy in your home. You will need to take a much more active approach to cleansing.

When our son was a teenager, he began to wake in the middle of the night struggling to breathe, gasping until he vomited violently. Multiple doctors found no physical reason for his episodes but prescribed an inhaler just in case he had another episode. When you're jolted out of bed several times a night in panic as your son chokes and gags, "just in case" is not enough. I confided in a dear friend who I knew was attuned to spiritual things. She wrote a prayer on the back of an envelope for me and we began to pray it every night before bed. Every night that we remembered to pray this prayer, our son slept peacefully. If we forgot, he would wake gasping for breath. After a few weeks, the episodes stopped and they have never returned.

This prayer (written below) holds no magic in itself. It's power lies in declaring spiritual truth and inviting God to protect your loved ones. Over the years, we've used this prayer to combat frightening dreams, to ease chronic insomnia and to clear the occasional sense of something unfriendly in the house. Most recently, we shared this prayer with a friend's husband who knew that a curse had been placed on him by an angry family member. His night terrors disappeared immediately.

As the caretaker of your home's sacred space, you have the authority to address these more serious issues from a position of spiritual strength. God has entrusted you to protect and bless those who live in your home; therefore you have the right to clear out evil, unwanted energies or spirits that disrupt your home.

If you do not feel like you have enough experience to stand against an evil presence, please contact a pastor or other spiritual leader for help in assessing the situation and reclaiming your home as a place of peace and safety. You do not need to feel embarrassed to ask for help. The unseen realm is very real. A wise and caring spiritual leader will take your concerns seriously and offer resources to help.

Protecting Your Home From Evil

- Walk Your Property – Many people find it helpful to actually walk around the perimeter of the property while praying. You may also want to walk through your house and pray in each room. By doing this, you are speaking into the atmosphere of each space, verbally cleansing and establishing the boundaries of your space – both physically and spiritually.

- Know Your Limitations – If you live in an apartment complex with many others, you do not have the spiritual authority to cleanse the entire property (unless you own the complex). You can still pray protection over your specific apartment, yard, patio, parking place, etc. You can certainly pray FOR your apartment complex and your neighbors, but it is not your place to try to exert any spiritual authority over them.

- Invite Others – When it comes to spiritual matters, there is strength in numbers. Invite your partner, a close friend or spiritual mentor to join you in praying through your home. Many people find comfort in the scripture that states "where two or three gather in my name, there am I with them."[8] If the presence in your home feels very dark or persistent after your initial attempts to cleanse your home, please do not try to stand against it alone.

- Know Your Strength – Whether you're experiencing a strong negative energy or an actual demonic spirit, the answer is the same: the power of God's truth and love. You do not need to be afraid. You are the spiritual authority in your home and therefore, you have the right to claim that home as a safe and peaceful place. Use the following prayers to pray for protection:

Prayer for Spiritual Protection

"As the spiritual leader of this home/family, I stand in my God-given authority and command any evil or unclean spirit or entity to leave this home and property immediately. Any previous invitation or claim that

you have had on this property or home is hereby canceled and broken through the power and authority of God. No evil is welcome here. Through the power of God, I place a spiritual hedge of protection around my home, my land, all vehicles and every person who dwells here. (You can name each one if you want.) I ask the angels of God to stand guard over this place and to ward off any evil that comes near. I give thanks that my home is safe and blessed. I declare today that the Kingdom of Heaven is welcome here on earth in my home."

Bedtime Prayer for Spiritual Protection:

"As we go to bed tonight, I pray in my God-given authority as the spiritual leader of this home. I ask the angels of heaven to stand guard around this and around each member of this family as we sleep. I present _____ (name each family member) and place a spiritual hedge of protection around our minds, our bodies, our spirits, our emotions and our dreams. I declare that no harm can come near us and nothing can disturb our sleep except what is allowed by our loving God. I give thanks that we will rest well and rise refreshed in the morning - ready to serve our world."*

*sometimes God will wake us to pray or will allow a troubling dream to send us a message.

Summary of Cleansing Section

1. Our homes gather both physical and spiritual dirt. Every person who enters a home leaves behind traces of their history and energy.

2. DUST - Energy is the invisible substance that forms our universe including your body and the atmosphere around you. As you move through your day, internal reactions ebb and flow in direct response to your choices and experiences. You emit energetic vibrations that others can sense and react to. A consistent dominant energy literally shapes the lives of those who share your home.

3. CRITTERS - Once a critter gets inside your home, it settles in and builds a home for itself. Unseen, emotional critters represent the ways in which another person's issue or energy invades your mind and emotions. Openings can occur through relationships, news or social media. A large part of your role is screening what and who has access to your precious home.

4. CLUTTER - Clutter represents a pattern of behavior – the result of a series of small, seemingly innocent decisions that nurture the very emotional energies you don't say you don't want. Clearing emotional clutter takes time because you are actually reprogramming your brain and resetting the chemical/hormonal code of your body.

5. COSMETIC - Homes have both a physical and spiritual past. If you begin experiencing unusual emotions, you may be tuning into the energy or vibration of past residents. Actively cleansing and blessing your sacred space not only benefits you but will also leave a wonderful legacy for the next occupants of your home!

6. COMPANY - Sometimes, especially in an older home, you sense that you are not alone in your space. You live surrounded by the spiritual realm. Spirits become more active when there is a change or disruption in the home such as a new owner, a major renovation or a new baby. As you clearly and respectfully establish your role as the spiritual care-taker for your family's space, any opposition or confusion should calm down.

7. CRISIS - Occasionally, a home's sacred space can contain more serious spiritual issues. As the caretaker for your home, you have the right to clear evil, unwanted energies or spirits that disrupt your home. Do not feel embarrassed to ask for help. A wise and caring spiritual leader will take your concerns seriously and offer resources to help.

May you have
Walls for the wind
And a roof for the rain,
And drinks beside the fire

Laughter to cheer you
Those you love near you,
And all that your heart
may desire

CELTIC BLESSING

PART 3

Blessing

Curled on that pile of dirty laundry so many years ago, I felt exhausted, hopeless and broken. I had no energy to even ask the right questions or to reach out for answers. My dream of a peaceful, loving home lay crumpled around me as surely as the mounds of smelly clothes under me. In those moments of despair, any expectation of "must" or "should" or "10 steps to a happy life" felt unbearable.

As I begin this section of the book, I feel myself treading cautiously. Tip-toeing slowly down those basement stairs toward my younger self.

She's so sad.

So disillusioned.

So angry.

So bone tired.

Aware that saying the wrong thing will do more harm than good, I gently reach out my hand to touch her shoulder. With wisdom that's grown from many more years of life, I whisper to her …

And to you …

"I see how hard you're trying to make it all work.

Rest awhile and then, when you're ready, let me show you a different way."

Remembering Blessing

"**D**o you know how to do a home blessing?"
When my daughter asked this question (in case you didn't read the introduction!), I'm sure she envisioned a simple, once-and-done blessing that would make her new apartment feel better. Sitting down at my computer to email her, that's exactly what I planned to send.

A few meaningful phrases. A heartfelt prayer. Light a candle. All is well.

The longer I wrote, the more my heart connected to humanity's longing for home in a world where stress, anxiety and depression rage at epidemic levels. We need more than a few words or a ceremony performed on a special day. Our bodies and spirits crave a haven. A way of life that centers around an age-old practice. The practice of Blessing.

For centuries, Blessing held a place of honor in cultures around the world. Ancient people groups experienced little separation between the physical and spiritual worlds. Regardless of continent, ethnic origin or religion, they built their daily lives on a foundation of deep respect for powers and forces beyond the world they could see or touch.

History records blessings from almost every culture - Jewish, Celtic, Asian, Native American, African and others. Woven throughout the fabric of each day, blessings accompanied the rising of the sun, preparing meals, building cooking fires, planting and harvesting crops, greeting a stranger, caring for the sick and lying down to sleep at night. Carefully crafted ceremonies marked significant life transitions such as the birth of a child, a young man's coming of age, embarking on a journey, going to war, taking a spouse or crossing in death. The most cherished blessings were passed from generation to generation through sacred writings or verbal repetition.

We may dismiss the idea of an angry god destroying crops or an appeased god granting victory in battle as outdated, pagan and fear-based. But one thing is clear: for centuries, entire societies centered their lives around belief in a world beyond the physical realm. Whether cursing their enemies or blessing their loved ones, they instinctively recognized and demonstrated what science now confirms: our thoughts, words, and the intentions behind them hold tremendous power.

How did we move from such daily intimacy with Blessing to its becoming a foreign concept in modern society? What changed?

Simply put, we got too smart for the "old ways." Advancements in technology, communication and industry impacted every area of modern life. We moved from growing and gathering our food to consuming mass-produced foods that can be delivered to our doorstep with a few clicks on our computer screens. Instead of walking or riding an animal to the nearest village, we can now fly to any spot on the globe in mere hours. Young men who once inherited the trade of their father and grandfather now choose from countless employment options. Young women enjoy active lives and careers without the societal expectation that they will marry at 13 or 14 and bear a dozen children. Multiple generations of one family seldom live under the same roof. Instead of sharing daily life in communities, our children now scatter across the globe to build lives based on core values of independence and individuality.

Lifestyles weren't the only significant change. Scientific exploration and discovery opened our eyes to astounding revelations about our world. As our knowledge of the physical world grew, the unseen, spiritual world seemed less legitimate. Less sophisticated. Less real.

We found ourselves forced to choose opposite banks of an ever-widening chasm. On one side rallied those who defined "real" as only that which could be proven, measured, calculated, categorized and observed in a laboratory. On the other side, those who still believed in a spiritual world retreated to the safety of sanctuaries. Worship became relegated to specific days of the week and sacred rituals performed by priests and ministers. Centuries of integrated tradition faded away under the glare of bold new ideas and ways of living.

All of which brings us to our current chapter in history. Several generations of physically- oriented living have taken their toll. Even a quick glance at the news, social media or the top 40 music hits reveals the restlessness, longing, depression, anger and emptiness that saturates our modern lives. We reach for a glass of wine, a remote control, a credit card, a cupcake, the keys to the car ... anything to keep us from feeling the ache inside.

Outwardly, our bodies are far more skilled, smart, sexy, sophisticated and successful than any generation in history.

Inwardly, our spirits starve for something more.

Progress has isolated us from one another, stripping our lives of deeper purpose and disconnecting us from the rich, ancient ways that once nourished us. In our quest to advance, we've come so far that we no longer know the way back.

Remember our soul questions? *Do I belong? Am I safe? Does my story matter?*

Finding answers to these soul questions has been further complicated by the conflict between science and religion. We've been taught to demand concrete evidence, proven track records, statistics and FDA approved solutions. Anything less is "woo woo." Faith in forces or realities beyond our physical world is dismissed

89

as a crutch that only the weak need. Yet we lay awake at night, torn between our logical minds and the growing ache in our spirit. An inner voice whispers "there has to be more to life than this cycle of work, eat, sleep, repeat." Political, religious and cultural divisions make it difficult to find common ground. Few messages can bridge all of these gaps and resonate with our true hearts.

When I grow quiet and sit with my own questions and longings, a deep and comforting truth saturates my awareness: **All humanity has been given common gifts.**

Every morning, the sun rises to warm every land and when it sets each evening, it displays its glorious colors for all to enjoy. Rain falls to nourish both the just and the unjust. Flowers bloom in the yards of the kind and the cruel. A baby's smile melts both the caring and the calloused heart.

In the same way, Blessing stands refreshingly apart from the controversies, power struggles, and dogma that divide us. It is one of our commonly shared gifts. While certainly holy and mysterious, Blessing does not dwell exclusively within the walls of cathedrals and monasteries. Although it enjoys a rich history of tradition, Blessing is neither outdated nor unsophisticated. While possessing incredible power, Blessing is offered equally to a beggar or a king. Connecting both the spiritual and physical worlds, Blessing resonates with all who desire a more meaningful way to live.

The memory of our true home still echoes deep within our being. Blessing invites us to remember and reconnect to our spiritual home. As we relearn the lifestyle of Blessing, we will once again nurture both body and spirit and create a healing legacy for future generations.

Blessing Basics

As Blessing has faded from our modern lives, we are left with many questions. What exactly is Blessing? Who is allowed to bless? Do I need holy water? What if I get it wrong? What should I say or do? How can I add one more thing to my hectic life?

We will examine all of this in depth, but let's begin with some Blessing Basics that should set your mind at ease:

- There is no "wrong" way to bless. A blessing is always just that. A blessing. No one in history has ever been hurt by a blessing so don't worry. You can't mess this up!
- Anyone can bless. You don't need a theological license or degree. No holy water necessary!
- The benefits of Blessing are scientifically sound. No need to check your brain at the door. (More on this in later sections)
- Blessing can be customized to match your available energy and time. Maybe all you can muster is a sticky note on your bathroom mirror. Or you may design a beautiful room-by-room ceremony. Either way, you live in a blessed home!
- Just as your physical home has its own color scheme, decorating style and rhythms of daily routine, your unseen home also has an emotional theme, a style of atmosphere and patterns of behavior. You can choose the kind of home you desire.
- You don't have to make Blessing happen. Your job is simply to select the blessings your home needs, "place the order," and anticipate their arrival with joy and gratitude.
- You are uniquely equipped to choose the right blessings for your home. You originated from purest Love – the exact kind of love that your home needs. Although you may often

feel overwhelmed, confused and cluttered, deep inside is a place where your spirit remembers when wholeness, beauty and pure love were your "normal." As you grow quiet and draw forth a blessing from this place, you become a conduit to connect heaven and earth.

Blessing Defined

When you hear the word "blessing," what comes to your mind? If we could share our answers over a cup of tea, we would discover how our unique life journeys have shaped our understanding, values and beliefs. To you, Blessing may be the prayer your family said before dinner. Or a religious ritual performed in a beautiful cathedral with stained glass and candles. Perhaps you envision a spiritual pilgrim chanting before a mountain top shrine. Or an act of kindness performed to help someone in need. Some of us may have never thought deeper than the standard "bless you" we offer when someone sneezes!

As you can see, there are many ways to experience Blessing. Even the Merriam-Webster dictionary offers seven definitions ranging from spiritual consecration to praising someone to invoking protection or well-being.

When I first tried to describe Blessing, I quickly realized that a thousand flowery words would still not capture its essence. So let's keep it simple:

Staying with the theme of home, we will define Blessing as **decorating the sacred space of your home.**

Blessing is the spiritual equivalent of quality furnishings, beautiful fabrics, warm lamplight and a soft blanket of belonging wrapped around yourself at the end of a long day. You've done the hard work of cleansing and preparing a beautiful empty space that echoes with promise and possibility. What you do next matters.

Imagine that you receive the keys to your new home. Opening

the door with excitement, you carry in your cleaning supplies and scrub the place from top to bottom. Once everything sparkles and smells divine, you breathe a big sigh of delight and plop down in the middle of the bare floor. "Ahhh ... home, sweet home!"

Sound a little uncomfortable?

Unless you're the minimalist-of-all-minimalists, your obvious next step would be to move in your furnishings, rugs and artwork. You would create a beautiful space filled with meaningful items that met your needs and expressed your personal style. For most of us, that's the fun part!

If you wouldn't consider living on a bare floor, why would you choose to dwell in a barren spiritual space? If you wouldn't allow your grass to grow thigh high or your roof to leak, why would you knowingly allow your spiritual home to fall into a state of abandonment and disrepair?

You wouldn't.

And yet we do. The good news is that with awareness comes the power to do better.

Doing Better

When I set up my first home, bridal registries and online ordering were still over a decade in the future. Brides were at the mercy of their wedding guests' tastes which usually aligned perfectly with that week's blue light specials at the local Kmart. Unpacking my wedding gifts, I discovered that I had scored six new skillets, several identical candy dishes and a small mountain of mushroom motif dish towels! (Mushrooms are tasty, but what designer ever thought they were a lovely décor choice?)

Unfazed, I cobbled together my random assortment of gifts, adding in a second-hand green flowered couch, towels and sheets in a half-dozen colors I hadn't chosen and heavy gold drapes inherited from my grandmother-in-law. I placed cheery tulip dishes in the cupboards and hung a wooden decoupage of praying hands over the mantel of our fake fireplace. I certainly wasn't winning any decorating awards. (In my defense, HGTV and Pinterest hadn't been invented yet either!)

I smile at the memory, knowing that I did the best I could with what I had. Despite the shudder-worthy décor, the flimsy walls of that rusty-teal-and-white mobile home resounded with friends, family, laughter, hard work and dreams of a better future.

Slowly but surely, changes came. We saved enough money to buy a soft blue carpet for the bedroom. Ahhh ... I still remember how luxurious it felt to sink my feet into it every morning. Next, we tried our hand at renovating the bathroom – the wallpaper fell down three times before we succeeded. Finally, we replaced the gold drapes with creamy lace-edged curtains. With each new decision based on my own decorating tastes, my little home began to feel more like "me."

Too often, the sacred space of our homes resembles the confusing hodge-podge of my first home. We find ourselves surrounded by patterns of behavior and belief that we didn't intentionally choose.

> ## The centerpieces of our spiritual décor may be inherited or gifted to us by significant people who passed on what was meaningful or helpful to them.

When we are young, inexperienced and unsure of our own beliefs, we tend to be heavily influenced by others. We gather a little of this and a little of that. Traditions that feel ingrained in our bones. Values modeled by people we admire. Concepts we've read. Ideals promoted by society. Lessons we've learned.

Or we do the opposite and run hard and fast away from the ideas and opinions of others, determined to forge our own path. Some of us build an entire life on the foundation of our refusal to be like those who've hurt us.

Either way, we cobble it all together and hope for the best. After a few years, most of us find ourselves staring at the bleak reality that our lives and our homes feel nothing like what our younger self envisioned. When you look at your spiritual home, remember the wise words of Maya Angelou,

> ## "Do the best you can until you know better.
> ## Then when you know better, do better."

You have done the best you could with the time, energy, and knowledge you've had. Now, you've accumulated the spiritual understanding, experiences and resources necessary to move to the next level. You possess the power to make different choices based on your own needs and desires. Just as my physical home evolved over the years, your unseen, spiritual home can transform into a healthier, more beautiful environment.

Where do you begin? It's simpler than you may think.

If someone handed you a catalog filled with the finest home goods and said, "Order whatever you want for your house, and by the way, money is no issue," you would know exactly what to do. You wouldn't make excuses about being too busy to shop. Nor would you waste time worrying that you wouldn't get it right. You would flip through those pages with a huge smile, eagerly choosing items that you loved and needed.

A few days later, delivery trucks would roll up to your doorstep with packages of all sizes and shapes. Unrolling rich colorful rugs, hanging tasteful drapes, grouping comfortable furniture, arranging fresh flowers, lighting fragrant candles, and stocking your pantry shelves with delicious and healthy foods, you would keep pinching yourself in joy at such an incredible gift. No one would have to tell you twice to fill your home with the very best choices for yourself and your family!

You possess a beautiful "design book" of blessings.

As you turn the pages, you see that it is filled with infinite, abundant and glorious options. Hope. Joy. Courage. Kindness. Beauty. Serenity. Gratitude. Rest. When it comes to the sacred space of your home, you no longer have to accept the hand-me-down ideas and beliefs of others. You can finally choose what you want, what feels right, what your spirit craves and what your family needs.

Before we begin, take a moment to appreciate the hard work you've done. Close your eyes and picture your clean spiritual home.

Breathe in the peace. Allow your mind's eye to see how the sun slants across the fresh-swept floor. Smell the faint aroma of cleanser. Place your hand on the nearest wall – strong and steady – supporting you. Anything is possible in this empty space. You get to design your own delightful home.

Let's begin by discerning what blessings are needed.

Listening

Earlier, I shared the story of how serious illness led me to a doctor who knew how to listen to my body. He taught me that symptoms should never be ignored, disguised or simply relieved with medication. They deserve to be heard because they carry important messages. My body sent me some very uncomfortable clues designed to get my attention and to guide me to the areas of my body that needed to be healed.

Our homes send us clues as well. After all, home is where real life happens. Out in the world, we keep it together most of the time, navigating the stress of traffic, work deadlines, play dates and parental obligations with our professional, polished pretense intact. But the minute we walk through the door of our home, our authentic self lets down its hair, pulls on its sweats and dives into the nitty-gritty of home life. Whether we live alone or share space with others, home offers us the safety and freedom we need to "keep it real."

Real comes in all forms. Real joy. Real pain. Real frustration. Real excitement. Real tenderness. Real sarcasm. Real nurturing. Real withdrawal. Real exhaustion. Real dreams.

Within the walls of home, we are creating a real life – whether by chance or by choice.

For many years, I was doing a lot more surviving than thriving. Any family member, myself included, would have snorted at the idea that I would someday write a book about creating a peaceful home. Of our six family members, five of us were adopted children with deeply ingrained emotional patterns of rejection, abandonment and anger. Our wounds and struggles clashed in brutal ways. We didn't mean to hurt each other. Or maybe we did. Some days it was hard to tell.

My daughter and I share an ongoing joke about those difficult days. I tell her that she should have come with a warning label. She tells me that she had one but she was so cute that I forgot to read it! And she's right. I didn't know how to read the signs that were right in front of me – sometimes literally screaming in my face.

Wouldn't it be nice if situations and people came with warning labels? A "check engine" light on our emotional dashboard? A red flag waving to alert us that a situation nearing the point of break down? Even better, how about a guide for fixing life?

The wise Creator gave us exactly that.

Stress. Arguing. Panic. Exhaustion. Loneliness. Rage. Disgust. Grief. Anxiety.

Wait ... what?

Aren't those BAD things? Things to avoid? To suppress? To mask? To self-medicate? To over-compensate for? To reveal only to a professional therapist ... maybe?

No, dear heart. Each of these emotions acts as a messenger sent to bring awareness to the weak, tired and sick areas of your life. Areas that need attention and love. If you learn to listen to your home, you'll hear not only the struggle, but you'll hear something beautiful as well. Wafting like a chime on the wind, you'll hear echoes from your true home. Memories of a time and place where you experienced a different way of being.

> ### Every painful moment holds not only the soul questions that haunt you, but also the answers that heal you.

The secret to listening to your home lies as close as the nearest thing that bugs you! You wouldn't waste a doctor's time by telling him everything that felt good. You would march into the medical office with a list of symptoms. So go ahead. Grab a piece of paper and let your frustration out! This is one time that you don't have to feel guilty about seeing the glass as half empty.

What are the top five things that annoy or stress you right now?

Your partner never lifts a finger to help

Your loved one's addiction

Your credit cards are maxed

No one remembered your birthday

Your child is being bullied at school

Your friend keeps posting photos of her amazing vacations and you're stuck at home

You can't remember when you last had a good night's sleep

Your co-workers are back-stabbing you

Your marriage feels boring

Your kids are resembling disrespectful little brats (we know of course that they aren't!)

Normally, we consider the negative things in our lives to be … well, negative! However, when viewed through the eyes of Blessing, every broken, hurting, and hard place holds a powerful clue that becomes a tool for healing. Pain and struggle carry important messages that will guide you right to the blessings your spirit needs.

I hate to break it to you, but the things that annoy you are NOT the real issues.

The list you just compiled merely reveals the safe distractions you focus on to avoid deeper, more painful feelings like fear, jealousy, hopelessness or rejection. Focusing on these everyday messes makes as much sense as nagging about socks on the floor during a house fire or scum in the tub during a flood.

"Issues, what issues?" If you really want to heal your home, you have to stop pretending that everything is fine. Outwardly, you keep up appearances by packing your days with the distractions of activity, addiction and even accomplishment. But deep inside, you are not fooled.

Every cell of your body reverberates with your truth.

After years of avoiding the real issues, your spirit deserves to be heard and honored. It is time to listen to the "messages in the messes."

Pick one of the issues you listed and dig a little deeper.

What soul question lies beneath the surface emotion?

What part of you is trying to be heard?

What emotion are you avoiding feeling?

Perhaps you find yourself constantly irritated. The easy thing is to blame others for being on your last nerve. Have the courage to dig deep enough to uncover what lies beneath that irritability. Nine times out of ten, your real emotion is not irritation, but a sense of feeling alone, unheard, or taken for granted. You may be subconsciously grieving the loss of the way you thought your life would be. Your soul screams "Do I matter?" while the words coming out of your mouth are "NOBODY EVER LIFTS A FINGER AROUND HERE."

Once you have identified the message your emotions are carrying, it's time to choose the change you desire.

Biologist Bruce Lipton refers to humans as "a skin-covered Petri dish with 50 trillion cells inside."[9] As a walking Petri dish, you move through each day responding to the stimuli in your environment. Every cell in your body marinates in a concoction of the chemicals and hormones triggered by your dominant emotions. Perhaps to this point, your cells have been swimming in a soup of stress, exhaustion, anxiety, anger or depression that feels impossible to change. You shrug your shoulders and accept that "this is just who I am." I am shy. I am opinionated. I am bossy. I am anxious. I am OCD. I am a shopaholic. I am messy.

Not so fast! The second a scientist introduces a new substance into a Petri dish, everything shifts in response. As the environment changes, the cells within it adapt and change as well. A toxic substance causes the cells to weaken, struggle or even die while a nourishing substance creates the ideal environment for the cells to thrive.

You are not a helpless clump of cells forced to saturate in whatever is happening around you.

In the grand laboratory of life, you get to be both scientist and subject. If you don't like the environment or the results in your life, you possess the power to create change. When you speak a blessing, you introduce a healing element into your personal "Petri" dish. Immediately, the cells of your body respond by triggering healing chemicals downloads. The process of rewiring your brain and reprogramming the physiology of your body begins. As your inner biological environment changes, the energy of your body and spirit shifts. The ripples extend to the spiritual atmosphere of your home and impact the lives of those around you as well.

By changing the emotional, physical and spiritual environment of your "Petri dish," transformation can occur.

Just as you would choose beautiful furnishings and items to create a comfortable physical home, you will now choose nurturing and healing elements to fill the sacred space of your home. Each blessing you choose will change the environment of your home for the better.

Remember the list of things that bug you? Use these as clues to identify what blessings are needed. The famous Prayer of St Francis provides a beautiful example of how to begin:

"Where there is hatred, let me sow love;
where there is injury, pardon,
where there is doubt, faith,
where there is despair, hope,
where there is darkness, light,
where there is sadness, joy."

Every difficult situation or emotion offers an opportunity for you to act as an instrument of peace – infusing your home with love, pardon, faith, hope, light and joy. More than just pretty phrases to hang on your wall, this prayer reveals a formula for alchemy that can transform every area of your life.

Are you lonely? Bless your home with a sense of belonging, of feeling connected and cherished by others.

Does your life feel empty and meaningless? Bless yourself with purpose, satisfaction and fulfillment.

Does your body feel strung tight with stress? Invite the blessing of ease, peace and fun.

As you allow yourself to be honest about your true needs, you'll recognize the opportunity for Blessing everywhere you look. Forget being a shopaholic. You may find yourself becoming a Blessaholic!

The best part is that you don't have to manufacture anything. Every blessing you desire and need already exists. I like to imagine them held in a cosmic storehouse, just waiting to be ordered. When you choose from the "Catalog of Blessings," you'll never receive a limited inventory, backorder or sold out notification. No one will ever call you greedy. You can bless all day long and you'll never exhaust the supply of goodness available to you.

Listening to the "messages in the messes" will instinctively guide you to choose the sacred furnishings your home needs. Physically, your body longs to be restored and realigned with health. Spiritually, your soul longs to rest and reconnect with your true home. Blessing brings both worlds together in a beautiful, life-changing way.

In the next chapters, you will learn many ways to invite Blessing into your home. We will begin with incredible power of spoken words.

Why Words Matter

In the spring of 2018, IKEA performed an experiment designed to show the impact of spoken words.[10] Placed in the lobby of a school, two identical plants received the same soil, water and light. As much as possible, the researchers gave both plants equal opportunity to grow with one distinct difference: one plant was chosen to receive words of praise while the other plant was forced to listen to a steady stream of insults.

School children participated in the experiment by telling the "blessed" plant that it was strong, beautiful and healthy. They also lined up to call the "cursed" plant names like stupid, ugly and worthless. At the end of thirty days, the results astounded everyone. The complimented plant thrived while the bullied plant showed clear signs of wilting and brown leaves.

Why did the children's words affect the plants? What strange power lies within the tongue?

According to Genesis, the Book of Beginnings, our physical world was "formless and empty" until the voice of Spirit pierced through the darkness with the first recorded words, "Let there be light."[11] And there was light. Reading further, each phase of creation unfolds through the simple words "Let there be ..." Oceans, lands, mountains, stars, mammals, fish. Over and over, the Word drew forth visible form from invisible void.

Skeptics dismiss the biblical account of creation as unscientific, mythical and at best merely symbolic. However, recent findings in the fields of quantum physics, epigenetics and neuro-science confirm that the words we speak, flowing from our thoughts and empowered by our dominant emotions, hold creative power. Our universe is so intricately connected that the simplest action sets in motion a ripple effect of reactions. Although usually unaware of our role, we actively participate in creating the world we experience. One of the main ways we shape our environment is through our words.

Spoken words carry such power that the book of Proverbs calls gentle words a "tree of life" and warns that a "deceitful tongue crushes the spirit."[12] Another passage teaches that "life and death are in the power of the tongue."[13] The IKEA plants would agree.

Simply put, what is spoken, becomes.

A truth with both miraculous and terrifying implications.

From the intimacy of the womb through the formative years of childhood … through the drama of adolescence into the exploration of young adulthood … from the rat race of family and career into the slow, settled habits of old age … our entire lives form around words.

Words spoken to us.

Words spoken about us.

And most importantly, words spoken by us.

Each of us can recall words spoken decades ago that still linger in our memory. Both positive and negative words influence our daily choices and may even shift the entire course of our life. In my own life, a careless comment, "You have really wide hips for such a little thing" threw me into a three year long eating disorder. Years later, the intentional jab of an angry child, "You're not my mother" triggered my own abandonment issues and led to deep depression.

On the positive side, a man I highly respected told my high school class, "Every young woman should develop a marketable skill." His words inspired me to study office management, skills which I use every day in my businesses. While writing this book, a friend's encouragement, "You paint pictures with your words," keeps me returning to my desk when I feel like giving up.

Amy Jae

Like the words spoken to the plants in the IKEA experiment, the words in our lives either nurture us, producing growth, strength and life. Or they deplete us, causing us to wither, lose heart and simply exist.

While all words matter, the earliest voices ring the loudest.

Your parents, siblings, babysitters, teachers and even childhood friends played vital roles in forming your views about yourself and life. In fact, you tuned so strongly to these early voices that their messages literally became part of your physiology. Survivors of childhood trauma display notably different brain functions and body chemistry than those who grew up feeling loved and nurtured.

Imagine that you are three years old, leaning against the soft warmth of your mother. She cuddles you close and whispers against your hair, "You're so precious. Mommy loves you!" Now imagine that your mother is stressed and running late to an important appointment. As your three-year-old self struggles with a stubborn shoe, she grabs you roughly by the arm. "Come on! I don't have time for this. You drive me CRAZY!!"

In each scenario, your mother's words spark an electrical, chemical, and energetic reaction. With each word, neurotransmitters carry positive or negative signals that surge to every organ, tissue and cell of your body, creating an immediate shift in your biological landscape. These changes can be observed and measured with scientific instrumentation.

In her book, "Habits of a Happy Brain," Loretta Graciano Bruening tells us that brain synapses are developed in two ways: REPETITION, which develops a synapse gradually. And EMOTION, which develops a synapse instantly.[14] Your dominant emotional state as a child wired your brain to survive in the exact type of environment in which you lived.

If your mother had a random bad day amid many loving days, the negative impact would be outweighed by the abundance of pleasant emotions. But if you spent your childhood days immersed in stress, anxiety, arguing or danger, your brain developed neural super highways to carry messages of depression, anger, criticism, fear, and frustration in a split second to all parts of your body.

Over time, these messages and impulses became deeply ingrained. You built your life around what felt normal to you. If your childhood experiences taught you that life is negative, difficult, painful, unfair or scary, you probably don't feel quite right when things go well. You try to anticipate the next crisis and live on guard, knowing that it won't be long until something goes awry. In fact, you may purposely pick a fight or self-sabotage just to get things back to your usual level of chaos. At a subconscious, cellular level, you need regular doses of fight or flight, stress and drama to replenish the chemicals that feel familiar to you.

On the other hand, if you grew up surrounded by stability, nurture, kindness and encouragement, the neurological activity of your brain will follow a very different pattern. You'll literally be hard-wired to expect and seek regular downloads of feel-good chemicals and hormones. Your "normal" will be a sense of love, security, hope, peace and good humor. You'll instinctively trust others more easily and embrace more joy and beauty in your day. Overall you feel certain that life can be meaningful and fulfilling. When things go wrong, you'll instinctively return to your familiar set point of well-being as quickly as possible.

It doesn't seem quite fair does it?

As you can see, spoken words form the foundation for our lives. Words we didn't have the luxury of choosing! By the time we become self-aware enough to desire change, we often feel trapped in patterns of thought, emotion and behavior set in motion decades earlier. In fact, by age seven, a child's brain has developed enough life experiences to form the way he or she will view the world for many years to come.

You may be reading this as an adult and thinking, "I can't go back and undo my childhood. Am I doomed?"

Absolutely not!

Remember the Petri dish? A scientist in a lab can change the environment of cells and create new responses simply by introducing a different substance. You're either going to keep reinforcing your toxic thoughts or begin creating new healing thoughts. Given the choice (which you are!), it makes the most sense to introduce the blessings you desire into your environment.

You have the choice to weaken and overwrite the old words and thoughts by introducing new healing messages.

With intention and repetition, you can rewire your "path of least resistance" brain activity, reverse your learned reactions and create a new emotional set point for your life. Creating lasting change through repetition takes time and patience and we are notoriously impatient people. When you connect the repetition of spoken blessings to a positive emotion, changes in your brain and body can occur instantly.

Read each of these phrases and take a moment to FEEL the emotion behind each blessing. Imagine joy saturating your body, calming your breathing, releasing the tension in your jaw, your shoulders, your chest. Feel sadness lifting a little. See light streaming through the darkness that seems so thick. Feel that light radiating out from you into the atmosphere of your home.

"Where there is darkness, light."

"Where there is sadness, joy."

Through your words and the power of emotion, you've just unleashed a new biological response. Subtle at first, a new reality has begun to form. The phrase "Let there be …" still carries creative force to draw the visible from the invisible in your life.

As a child, you held little control over the environment of your home. The adults in your life decided the tone, the energy and activity levels that surrounded you. Even if you were a little terror who ruled the roost, you no doubt acted out because you did not feel safe enough to trust the adults in your life to be in charge of you.

Now you're the adult. No one else controls the environment in which your cells swim. Not your unreasonable boss. Not your irritable spouse. Not your whining three-year-old. Not your psychotic neighbor. Not even your childhood abuser. While other people certainly have an impact, you get to decide how you will allow those people to affect your well-being. Just as you selected the style of couch you sit on and the color of the rug at your feet, you now have the power and responsibility to fill your sacred space with "furnishings" that bring you comfort, joy and enable you to thrive.

The place to begin lies about two inches beneath your nose!

Watch Your Mouth

Ear-splitting screams rang through the aisles of the grocery store. The toddler banging his sippy cup against the cart was clearly beyond soothing. Avoiding the eyes of the other shoppers, his father finished paying his bill and headed for the parking lot where he struggled to buckle the thrashing child into his car seat. The woman loading her groceries into the next car noticed the young man's lips moving and heard him calmly repeating, "Everything is ok, Jimmy. Everything is ok, Jimmy. Everything is ok, Jimmy."

Impressed with his calmness under such stress, the woman waited until the car door closed, muffling the child's wails. With a warm smile, she said, "I know how hard children can be at that age. I want to commend you for doing such a remarkable job of reassuring Jimmy. You're a great dad." The young man looked confused for a moment and then chuckled, "I wasn't talking to the kid. I'm Jimmy!"

We live surrounded by many voices. Messages from our past, our present and even our future pull us in many directions. We should do this. We shouldn't do that. We succeed if we achieve this. We fail if we miss that mark. This brand. That method. This opinion. That review. The chaos of voices exhaust, confuse and even control us until we discover the incredible power that we possess. The power to talk to ourselves!

Your current life has formed upon layers of messages from others, but one voice holds the greatest potential to shape your life.

*Cutting through the chorus of all the other voices, the voice that directs your life more than any other is **your own voice.***

Your mind may be filled with deeply ingrained thoughts that replay day and night. You may find yourself acting out in decades-old coping mechanisms. You may feel that no one understands the difficulty of the situation you find yourself in. It may seem impossible to climb back up from the dirty laundry pile in the basement and find any joy in life.

When all of these negative messages wail in your ears, remember Jimmy calmly reassuring himself. You can speak to yourself in ways that make a real difference. Your tongue holds the "power of life and death" to create a new reality of health and wholeness in your own life and in your home.

What is spoken ... **becomes.**

Pay attention to the words you speak in the course of a day. How do you talk about yourself? Your life? Your friends and family? Here are some phrases I frequently hear coming from my own mouth and the mouths of those around me:

"I'm exhausted."

"We're broker than broke."

"Nobody appreciates what I do around here!"

"I'm overworked and underpaid."

"If it isn't one thing, it's another."

"I hate my life."

"I'm surrounded by idiots."

"I have the worst luck."

"I can't do this anymore."

"I never catch a break."

If it were possible to connect you to a meter showing the biological impact of these phrases in your body, you would probably clap your hand over your mouth in shock. Few of us would intentionally choose to curse ourselves and yet dozens of times a day, we do just that! Our words create negative responses in our bodies, reinforcing all the old messages of pain, frustration and anger. This energy ripples out to charge the atmosphere around us with a vibration of invisible (but very real) crud.

The words you speak are not by chance – They provide clues to the way your brain is currently wired.

"The mouth speaks what the heart is full of!"[15] Words reveal the thoughts, emotions and beliefs that lie buried inside. If you want to know what kind of furnishings currently fill your sacred space, just listen to yourself speak. Then ask yourself, "Is this the kind of life I want?"

The good news is that your brain and your beliefs can change! Multiple studies are showing the power of thought to relieve lifelong emotional struggles and to even reverse serious disease. When you add the power of the spoken word, the effects become even more stunning.

Your brain may contain neural superhighways dedicated to depression. On your darkest days, you feel incapable of mustering a single positive thought. But the moment you speak the words, "Let there be joy," your reality shifts a little. A tiny trickle of endorphins is released. The first layer of a neural "joy track" is laid. A track you can continue to build on with every word of Blessing.

When you speak a blessing into your life, three powerful things happen.

- You choose to think a different thought which in itself is incredibly powerful.
- You back up the new thought with action by speaking aloud.
- You receive the blessing by hearing it coming back into you from the most powerful voice in your life ... your own voice.

You benefit as both the giver and the receiver of Blessing!

Once a blessing leaves your lips, it resonates and ripples outward, shimmering through your sacred space. Changes begin immediately. Thoughts change. Responses change. Body chemistry changes. Energy changes. Demeanor changes. Your impact on those around you changes. Their response to you changes. The atmosphere changes. Your home changes. Your life changes.

Word by word. Moment by moment. Your life story can be rewritten.

You don't have to live with the emotional/spiritual equivalent of an old broken-down twin bed when your spirit desires a beautiful, hand-carved, king-sized one. Every issue or obstacle presents an opportunity to place an order for something new and beautiful. Every place of pain or anxiety becomes a portal through which heaven can touch earth.

No wonder our ancestors wove blessing throughout their daily routines. Through the history of written blessings, we see people from every continent, religion and walk of life engaged in the practice of Blessing. They blessed everyone from their children to the stranger on the road. They cherished the gift in everything from the rising of the sun to the grains baked into their bread.

I envision a world where people once again speak blessings all day with generosity and joy! I've included many blessings in the back of the book to help you begin. As we've learned in this chapter, spoken words are powerful. But some situations require a more subtle approach.

The next chapter will show you how to bless your home without saying a word.

Unspoken Blessings

When the kids skip their afternoon nap, every mom knows that the evening holds the potential for disaster. On this particular evening, I didn't have the luxury of staying home and riding out the storm. I wrangled the girls into their car seats, bribing them with goldfish crackers. Driving to the church where my husband and I were youth leaders, I mentally prepared myself for the hours ahead.

The evening did not disappoint. Over 40 teens careened around the gymnasium as I supervised games, served snacks and listened to the usual complaints about friends, school stress and parents. Balancing my fussy baby on my hip, my head pounded almost as loudly as the music. Everyone seemed more rambunctious than usual that night. My toddler raced by with a teenager chasing her, both laughing hysterically. My stomach growled and my last nerve twanged ominously. As much as I loved this youth group (and I did), I felt relief as the door slammed behind the last teen.

Backing from my parking spot, my headlights illuminated a lone girl sitting on the curb. My heart dropped as I knew what this meant. Her parents were running late … again. Pulling alongside her, I weighed my options. If I waited with her, my whiny children would get to bed even later. If I invited her to wait for her parents at my home, she would witness the imminent bedtime chaos. Apparently, she was hoping for an invitation because she opened the back door and squeezed between the car seats before I could decide which option to offer.

A few moments later, we entered the house less than gracefully – keys dropping noisily, toddler lagging behind, baby sliding down my hip, diaper bag caught on the doorknob while I blocked the cat's escape with my foot. Clicking on the lights, I mumbled an apology for the mess we'd left behind when we scurried off hours earlier. My husband ran bathwater for our three-year-old while I changed the baby's diaper and warmed a bottle. Sobs of tired protest broke out in the bathroom. I think it was my daughter, but it could have been my husband!

Closing my eyes, I settled into the rhythm of rocking while my baby slurped her evening bottle. Across the room, my teenage charge curled up on the couch and wrapped a blanket around herself.

"I just love coming to your house. It's always so peaceful." She murmured with a long, contented sigh.

The rocking chair lurched as I snorted with surprise and disbelief!

Peaceful?? All I could see were the toys she almost tripped on, the overflowing laundry basket by the couch, the dirty dishes piled in the sink. The muffled wails still resounding from the bathroom seemed to emphasize the very obvious "not-togetherness" of my life.

Sitting shocked in the semi-darkness, my eyes fell on a single word presiding over all of the chaos.

P. E. A.C. E.

A few weeks earlier, I stood in the aisle of a craft store choosing those five wooden letters to paint as a little home décor project. From a hundred color options, I felt drawn to a bottle of soft sage green paint. The color looked like peace and my home needed peace. My children, adopted from difficult situations, needed peace. My husband, working two jobs while renovating our cramped house to make room for our growing family, needed peace. Struggling to juggle the demands of it all, I needed peace. I imagined that if I hung the word PEACE on our wall, it would somehow help..

And I believe it did.

Even surrounded by clutter and crankiness at the end of a long and frustrating day, my guest felt peace in my home. Gurgling contentedly in my arms, my baby felt peace. My energetic toddler, now listening to a bedtime story, felt peace. Amazed by the realization of it all, I felt peace.

Since that night, I have incorporated many subtle but powerful methods to bless my home. Blessing comes in many forms. What works for one person may feel awkward for another. You may be an introvert, not particularly spiritual or even a skeptic. Your partner or roommate may be unaware or not supportive of your new intention to care for your home's sacred space. Or perhaps your teenagers already consider you to be weird and would not even allow you to speak a verbal blessing over them. In some situations, it simply doesn't work to bless with words. Thankfully, you can bless your home without ever opening your mouth.

By consciously infusing Blessing into your daily routines, you can silently change the atmosphere of your home.

Think of someone you know so well that you can finish each others' sentences or hold an entire conversation with just a glance. The person you dare not glance at during an awkward moment because you'll both explode in inappropriate laughter. You know ... that friend! Unspoken blessings work in the same way.

Blessing and you go way back. Back to your spirit's true home where you experienced perfect love, peace and joy. Like old friends, your spirit shares a familiar connection with Blessing that doesn't require words. A simple thought, intention or action communicates your desire in an instant. Love. Hope. Rest. Courage. Whatever you need, Blessing eagerly responds to your invitation.

You don't even have to tell anyone what you're up to! As you choose to create a more peaceful, joyful environment, your loved ones will sense the difference and respond at a cellular level to the unspoken blessings. Their minds and bodies cannot help but align with the vibration you have chosen for your home. Even the toughest skeptic (and sometimes that's you!) will enjoy the benefits of living in a blessed home.

This morning, the final phrase from a McDonald's commercial caught my attention. "Joy Included." These two words caused me to stop what I was doing and turn toward the screen. Who doesn't want joy? Even the marketing experts at McDonald's understand the power of the blessing of joy! When we hold the intention of Blessing, even a hamburger becomes an opportunity to include a little extra splash of joy. Or hope. Or fun. Or serenity.

Guests arrive at our bed and breakfast expecting a clean room, a comfortable bed and a hearty breakfast. Any good innkeeper provides these basics, but my guests enjoy an atmosphere saturated with unspoken blessings. They don't know it, but every detail of our guest rooms has been designed with Blessing in mind - from the paint color to the scent of the soap to the book on the bedside stand.

As I make the beds, I whisper a blessing of relaxation and peace for those who will sleep there. We build the morning fire, brew the coffee and bake the muffins with the intention that our guests will feel cared for, energized and inspired for the day's adventures. And it works! Over and over, our guests tell us that they slept better than they have in months. They remark on the good energy in the house and write rave reviews about feeling refreshed and at home. They are receiving the benefit of a "joy included" mindset.

Lest you think I have a dream life ... there are days when I feel less-than-enthused about scrubbing another toilet, cooking for a guest with a finicky diet or being cheery first thing in the morning. Keeping the greater mission in mind motivates me through the days when I'd rather be laying on a beach. When I consciously infuse Blessing into my chores, they are transformed into acts of love. The atmosphere in my home becomes energized with joy and rest. I feel more fulfilled in my work and my guests leave with smiles on their faces.

You can do this in your own home. After you listen to the "messages in the messes," identify one or two specific blessings that your home needs. Using your five senses of sight, sound, smell, touch and taste, look for ways to invite these blessings. Without saying a

Amy Jae

word, you can reset and re-design your home's atmosphere 24 hours a day – even while you sleep!

Here are some ideas to get you started:

SIGHT

Throughout history, the practice of writing on walls, doorways, clothing and even skin has helped people to remember their truths. Marketing and advertising experts use the power of subtle clues, words and symbols to influence our thoughts and decisions. Have you ever noticed how many spas display words like RELAX or BREATHE on their walls? Simply reading these words signals your brain to release relaxing, peaceful chemicals through your body. When it comes to blessing your home through the sense of sight, you don't have to invest in costly artwork. These simple methods will work just fine:

- A "sticky" note on the bathroom mirror starts the day with a blessing.
- Buy block letters and paint them to spell out the blessings you want
- Change your account or WiFi passwords to reflect the blessings you desire. This is a great way to subtly bring Blessing into others' lives as well. When our daughter went through a few years of teenage attitude, we changed the log-in for the family computer to "sweetspiritgirl" as a friendly reminder of the vision we held for her! We've also used passwords that invited joy, abundance and family fun.
- Use the psychology of color to choose paint, bedding or accents that invite the blessings you wish to experience in your home. For a calm environment, decorate with greens and blues. Yellow or orange can spark joy, creativity, energy and fun. Purple works well to invite reflection or meditation. Red inspires passion, love and even aids digestion which is

120

why many restaurants use red and orange in their decor. Color engages the brain to create changes to mood, body chemistry and vibration - all of which greatly impact your home's atmosphere. We experienced a powerful shift toward peace when we repainted our daughter's hot pink room to a soothing sage green.

- Use photos or artwork to invite Blessing. Mirror neurons cause us to reflect what we see around us. Hang photos of your loved ones laughing joyfully or working together on a project. Display artwork of beautiful scenery, luscious foods or a meaningful memory to remind you to appreciate the blessings around you. Photos of extended family or a group of friends can ward off loneliness and disconnection by reminding you that you belong to a social group beyond your own small world.

- Create a Blessing Wall – Many homes already have a gallery wall with photos of family and friends. Take this concept deeper by using these photos as a reminder to bless each person as your eyes fall on their photo. If you don't have room for a wall of photos, create a collage for your desk or a special album/folder on your phone. Take a few moments each day to look at the faces of those you love, remembering how much they mean to you and consciously sending them love, joy, courage, etc.

- Print or hand write a meaningful quote, a favorite poem, Bible verse or blessing and frame it. You can select a different blessing for each room that represents your vision for that room.

- Hang a chalkboard in a prominent place and write a "blessing of the day" or change it once a week

- Collect items that represent specific blessings or memories. Decorate with rocks or seashells from a favorite vacation spot. Display a vase from your favorite aunt and keep it filled with fresh flowers. Each time you see these visual reminders, your brain reconnects to the emotions of that special place or person

- Written Blessings – Sometimes it is easier for us to express ourselves through writing. Leave notes on pillows, dressers, car dashboards or in backpacks. Notes of blessing may also be less awkward for the recipient because they don't have to respond on the spot. (Think teenager!) You can be assured these notes will be treasured as a tangible, visible sign of your love.

- Choose a piece of meaningful jewelry to remind you of a blessing. Because I struggle with feeling unloved, I wear three small rings that symbolize the past, present and future love that surrounds me. Every time I touch those rings, I remember that I am on a journey of love. A bracelet or necklace inscribed with words like "Believe," "Joy," or "Courage" can be a powerful tool for blessing. If you want to focus on a special blessing for your family, you could consider buying each family member a matching piece of jewelry.

- Tattoos provide a permanent reminder of a word, symbol or picture that holds great meaning for you. Obviously, this idea isn't for everyone, but a carefully chosen tattoo certainly makes a bold statement about a specific blessing that you desire to invite for the rest of your life.

SOUND

While technically not silent, using sound or music can adjust the atmosphere in a room faster than almost anything else. Soft jazz in a romantic restaurant creates quite a different mood than the pounding beats in a nightclub. The soft rhythm of rain on a roof brings a soothing sense of peace while the honking of horns or the persistent pounding of a jackhammer sets one's nerves on edge.

Used creatively, sound is a powerful tool of Blessing to create the home you desire.

- Create a Blessing playlist - Instead of listening to songs that reinforce your struggles, choose songs with lyrics that focus on what you desire - hope, peace and abundance. Play these songs in the car, while you work out, or in the kitchen while you cook. Music sets a tone so you could have several playlists – one for when you want to feel happy and tap your toes and another one for more soothing, serene moments. Fall asleep listening to words of encouragement or peace. Even while you sleep, the messages will be absorbed subliminally and inner shifts will occur.
- Choose healthy background noise – The sounds of our homes create the soundtrack for our memories. To this day, the sound of flapping laundry, the slam of a screen door or the tinkle of wind chimes represent home to me. Be conscious of the sounds in your home. Do you want your child to remember the constant blah blah blah of a TV in the background or to lie in bed listening to arguing voices? Create peaceful, fun sounds on purpose as a way of blessing your home.
- Bring nature's sounds into your home – If you live in the country, open the windows and welcome the melody of a bird, the babble of a brook or the rustle of leaves. If you live in the city or it's zero degrees outside, play one of the many YouTube nature sound videos with soothing ocean waves, the sound of rain or murmur of a brook. These sounds signal our brain that it is ok to relax resulting in the release of calming endorphins.
- Explore "frequency" music – Because music is an actual vibration, the combination of science and sound can be used to shift our own vibration. Songwriters and sound engineers create music using specific keys and tonal frequencies that

stimulate various brain functions. By playing these songs in your home, you can tune yourself to the frequencies of happiness, love, courage, healing, focus, and sleep. Many frequency recordings can be found on YouTube.

SMELL

The sense of smell connects intimately to our memories. Home can smell like coffee, a warm apple pie, freshly mowed grass, our mother's perfume, a familiar fabric softener or hot pavement after rain. By filling your home with smells that invoke comfort, nurture or joy, you can bless yourself and others without saying a word. This is a great method to use if you live with grumpy or uncooperative people. After all, everyone has to breathe!

— Bake – When you think of your kitchen as a center for healing, preparing food moves from a chore to therapy. Not only will you, the baker, be blessed, but everyone who walks through the door will say, "Ahhhh...." It's really hard to stay in a bad mood when there is a fresh loaf of bread cooling on the counter. If you're not into baking from scratch, use a cookie mix or frozen bread dough.

— Burn candles with homey scents – If you don't have the time or patience for baking, fill your home with good smells by burning candles with scents like apple pie, sugar cookie, banana bread or cinnamon spice. You can also choose fragrances that remind you of a special place or mood. Note – most air fresheners or plug-ins contain artificial chemical scents. Use natural scents and soy-based candles to avoid filling the air with toxins of a different sort.

— Explore Essential Oils – Not only are essential oils effective in cleansing your home, but they can also be powerful tools for opening minds and hearts to Blessing. The essences of each plant contain both physical and emotional healing properties. Diffusing an oil or wearing a few drops as a perfume stimulates the brain to release corresponding chemicals and hormones which create biophysical responses. Special blends of oils encourage Harmony, Hope, Joy, Courage, Peace and many other blessings. (For more information on essential oils, see the Resources at the end of the book.)

– Anoint your home – Many spiritual traditions recognize the practice of anointing a person or an object with oil for healing, cleansing and dedication. While you can purchase special oils for these purposes, remember that the oil itself does not hold the power. Even ordinary olive oil will do the job when you use it with intention and meaningful symbolism. Anointing can be a powerful way of consecrating your home as a sacred space. The most common places to anoint a home are the main entry door, the door frame of each room and all windowsills. You can also anoint the beds to invite peaceful sleep and the table where you share your meals. Many people feel that anointing represents protection. You are signifying that your home is a safe place where only the highest good is welcomed!

TOUCH

The importance and blessing of human touch cannot be overemphasized. Within moments of birth, hospitals place newborns on their mothers for skin-to-skin contact. Being held, cuddled and stroked provides incredible physical and emotional benefits for both mother and child. The early weeks and months of life lay the groundwork for our lifetime of social development and connection. Children who do not receive healthy, nurturing touch struggle to thrive. Those who experience inappropriate or abusive touch show measurable differences in their brain structure than their peers who live with loving touch. Even as adults, we need touch more than we realize. During our foster parent training, we learned that a human needs 12 touches a day just to maintain emotional health. How can you implement touch into your home as a form of blessing?

- Weave Touch Throughout the Day – Look for moments to make healthy touch a part of your daily routine. Exchange hugs when leaving or returning home. High-five your kids when they have a victory. Hold hands when you bless your meals. Cuddle during an evening movie. Take time for hugs and kisses as you tuck little ones in bed. You're probably already doing most of this, but doing it consciously adds an extra element of Blessing. By building touch into the rhythm of your day, you ensure that everyone, yourself included, experiences the many benefits and blessings of touch.

- Offer Touch for Comfort/Nurture – Sometimes there are no words to heal a hurting heart. In these moments, a hand on the shoulder, an extra cuddle or a long heartfelt hug can release a healing cascade within a loved one's body and soothe their spirit.

- Respectful Touch – Some people are very uncomfortable with touch – even as small children. This can be difficult if you're a hugger! Please respect the emotional and physical needs of your loved one. Forcing them to hug or cuddle will always do more harm than good. In addition, some people have a history of abuse that makes it difficult for them to relax when another person invades their personal space. If you live with someone who resists touch, look for gentle ways to offer the blessing of touch such as a quick pat on the shoulder, a fist bump or high five. Allow the other person to initiate physical contact and when you feel them pull away from a hug, release them immediately. Be sure to read the clues. If the person you want to bless seems non-receptive to touch, look for another way to bless them.

- Rock in your Pocket – Choose a special rock, crystal or a similar item and slip it in your pocket each morning. Throughout the day, touch it as a reminder to stay calm, choose joy, forgive, breathe, focus on abundance ... whatever blessing you need! You can also carve or paint a significant word on the rock. The touch of that rock returns your focus to your chosen blessing when you most need it.

- Use of Hands in Blessing – In faith traditions, it is a common practice to lay hands on the head or shoulders of the one being blessed. Holding hands while saying grace before a meal is another familiar way of blessing. The use of your hands in blessing represents giving or bestowing a powerful gift. It can be especially meaningful for significant occasions or milestone blessings.

- Massage or Reflexology – If you live alone or just aren't receiving the healing touch your spirit needs, consider asking a good friend to trade back, shoulder or foot rubs. You can also treat yourself to a professional massage or reflexology session. In addition to the many health benefits, your spirit will also be blessed with a sense of connection and being cared for by meeting your need for human touch.

- Cuddly Clothing – A special piece of clothing like a favorite sweatshirt, a snuggly bathrobe or thick, warm socks can convey the sense of being touched. Each member of my family owns a personal hand-made blanket from me. As they wrap these blankets around themselves, I envision them being held close when I can't touch them physically. Even if you're not crafty, your local fabric or craft store sells pre-cut kits with everything you need to make a simple fleece "tie" blanket in a favorite color or fun pattern that is meaningful to the recipient.

TASTE

We turn to comfort food for a reason! Familiar tastes connect us to fond memories and create a sense of belonging. Multiple times a day, you have the opportunity to feed yourself and your loved ones in a way that communicates nurture and care. When our emotional needs are met, the need to binge eat unhealthy foods subsides. Don't worry if you aren't a good cook. When prepared and served mindfully, even a simple bowl of oatmeal or a nicely arranged plate of sliced cheese and crackers can be an act of love and blessing.

- Plan to Succeed – Living in "no idea what's for dinner" mode causes stress and usually results in poor food choices. Nurturing your body and spirit is too important to be left to chance. When you prepare and shop from a simple menu, you eliminate much of the stress surrounding dinner and save money by reducing the number of times you eat out or buy overpriced processed foods. See Resources for some helpful meal planning websites.

- Eat as a Family – My childhood family ate dinner together every single night so it felt natural to continue the tradition with my own family. Over the years, our best, deepest and most hilarious conversations have taken place around the dinner table. Conversations that would not have happened if we didn't make the effort to sit down and eat at the same time. A startling number of families no longer share meals. In many homes, everyone "fends for themselves." Some members take food to their rooms while others sprawl out in front of the TV. Taking even 20 minutes to sit down together can make a huge difference in your family dynamic. Each person gets a chance to debrief about their day, tell a funny story and learn to honor one another through listening. Being heard is so rare these days that people are paying professional listeners. Family dinner is way cheaper than therapy!

- Eat Alone Well – Most of the single people I know dodge the loneliness of mealtime by eating on-the-go, skipping meals or snacking their way through the day. When they are at home, they eat while answering emails or binge-watching their favorite show. If you live alone, preparing delicious food, serving it attractively and savoring each bite with conscious gratitude may seem like a waste of time and energy. But please consider that the way you nourish yourself sends a powerful statement to your mind, body and spirit. You deserve to be nurtured. You deserve beautiful, healthy foods. You deserve to enjoy yourself. Light a candle. Put on some jazz. Give thanks and allow the love you show yourself to permeate the atmosphere of your home. For inspiration, read Daniel Halpern's classic poem, "How to Eat Alone."[16]

- Prepare Favorite Foods – Knowing and remembering a loved one's favorite foods conveys that you know and remember THEM. When you see a family member who seems sad or angry or stressed, offering a tasty snack or cooking their favorite dish can convey the unspoken blessing of caring and compassion. On several occasions when my daughter had shut herself in the bedroom for hours, her favorite dinner of BBQ meatballs drew her out and put a smile on her face again.

- Create Nourishing Traditions – Grandma's meatball recipe, pizza every Saturday night, hot chocolate during the first snowfall, a Christmas Eve cheese ball, ice cream cones on the last day of school and S'mores around a campfire may seem like simple things, but they create a nurturing foundation for life. Special food traditions provide structure, connection, and a sense of home base where loved ones can moor during the storms of life. Listen for the words, "but we always …." and make a mental note. You're being told that a certain tradition is meaningful. I felt this joy the first time my adult daughter asked for my sweet potato casserole recipe!

- Give Food Gifts – Thoughtful food gifts can break down barriers, bring cheer and provide a tangible sign that you care. I love the Jewish tradition of offering bread, salt and sugar as housewarming gifts. These gifts represent a blessing: "Bread so that you shall never know hunger. Salt so your life shall always have flavor. Sugar so your life shall always have sweetness."[17] Other food blessing traditions include taking meals to a sick friend, welcoming new neighbors with a casserole and sending birthday cupcakes to school with your child. If you know someone who struggles with loneliness or depression, a simple invitation to go out for pizza or ice cream shows that they are not forgotten or unappreciated. Even if they decline, they have been blessed by your thoughtfulness. Donating items for a charity bake sale or canned goods to your local food pantry reminds you that you have been blessed with more than you need. All of these gifts communicate Blessing to their recipients.

Bringing it all Together

Many of these unspoken blessings are already part of your life. You've been doing a lot of things right! Bringing greater awareness and intention to your common habits and choices allows you to weave a beautiful lifestyle of Blessing throughout each day. Let's see how this can work.

Perhaps you recognize a pattern of bickering and irritability among your family members. You don't want this vibration filling your home so you listen to the "message in the mess" and determine that your family hasn't had fun together in awhile. You want to shift the atmosphere from busyness and stress to connection and happiness. Using the five senses, you can design an entire evening to reverse the vibration of irritability.

SIGHT - Place a visual item that represents fun in a prominent spot. Perhaps a photo from a family vacation or a piece of wall art that says "The family that laughs together …." or "Home is my happy place."

SMELL - Light a candle or diffuse an essential oil such as "Joy" or "Harmony."

TASTE – Food is essential! Make some of your favorite foods – for tonight, focus on fun foods even if they aren't the healthiest. You can go back to salad tomorrow.

SOUND - Crank up some cheerful tunes and dance in the kitchen while you cook.

TOUCH - If your kids are young (or young at heart), plan games that incorporate touch, such as Twister, tag, a water gun or snowball fight or a backyard game of football or capture the flag.

If you live alone, tune into happiness with a funny movie, calling a friend (or your mom!) or a brisk walk around the neighborhood to get the endorphins flowing. End the evening with a savory treat like ice cream with crazy toppings or have fun making your own pretzels with a ready-made kit. In one evening, you've utilized every single sensory experience to align your body and spirit with the blessing of fun and happiness.

Struggle And ... Blessing

When we moved to the Adirondacks, our 120 plus-year-old home was a local historic landmark. We fell in love with its beautiful woodwork, wavy glass window panes, fascinating quirks and abundant character. This grand old home had everything we hoped for.

It also had issues.

No amount of scrubbing and sanitizing could erase the reality of a lifetime of wear. Deep scratches traced their way across the sloping floor. Cold winds whistled under the weathered doors. Cracked and peeling plaster made some walls look like road maps. Repairs could be made, but they would take time and cost thousands of dollars.

During the process of renovation, I had a choice to make. I could have complained and protested and refused to feel at home until the house met my standards. I could have been too embarrassed to invite anyone over. But frankly, we had a mortgage to pay and opening our doors to guests was a necessity!

So I hid the scratched floorboards under colorful rugs and blocked the drafty doors with rolled-up towels. I covered the beds with warm comforters, hung artwork on the cracked walls and served beautiful food under the flickering light of the old chandelier.

Even with scratched and sloping floors, drafty windows and scarred walls, our home is an award-winning bed and breakfast hosting thousands of travelers from around the world. Hundreds of online reviews use phrases like "beautiful," "peaceful," and "just what we needed." Ironically, the word "perfect" appears frequently!

Our home didn't have to be perfect in order to bless others. And neither does yours!

Your body and spirit also show the wear of a lifetime of human experience. Cracked and broken places allow the cold winds of fear and doubt to blow through your sleepless nights. You've learned hard lessons. Your heart has been broken. Your trust betrayed. Your security shaken. You have developed deeply embedded thought patterns, emotional responses and core beliefs. All of which now guide your daily decisions.

You too face a choice. You can resent these damages and blame others. You can refuse to fully live until you've fixed yourself enough – until you've lost that extra 20 pounds, paid off your school loans, raised the kids, organized the closets, met the right person, found the right career. You can stare at all that's wrong and scarred and ugly, wishing you had the resources to make the needed repairs.

Or through Blessing, you can begin to add beauty now.

Imagine an old wall pock-marked with chunks of missing plaster. Cracks cut across its surface and several layers of out-dated wallpaper peel away in strips. Now hang a carefully selected piece of art on that wall. Suddenly, you've changed the view. The old wall still exists, but now you see an old wall AND a lovely picture.

Blessing is the beauty, the comfort, the wisdom and the hope that we add to the struggle.

The struggle still exits, but we can change the view to include Blessing.

Take today for example – a much needed quiet day at the end of a long busy season of hosting guests. After the rare luxury of sleeping in, I ate a good breakfast and puttered about the house with no pressing agenda for the first time in weeks. The sun shone warmly as I took a walk to enjoy one of our last autumn days. Several of my children texted me and I enjoyed a phone call with my sister. I sent a few text messages of my own, wrote in my journal and read a chapter from an inspirational book. Dinner simmers in the crockpot, filling the house with great smells.

And yet my heart hurts.

Throughout the day, I have been shadowed by my old familiar companions of sadness and loneliness. Outwardly, nothing is wrong and yet an ache throbs just beneath the surface as it has for much of my life. This ache doesn't care if I'm alone or surrounded by people. It can claim the hours of a quiet day or intrude into a full schedule of work. At a cellular level, these emotions run deeply through my body. Their messages have carved wide pathways into my mind. My spirit sighs under the weight. Despite my desire for joy and connection, my life has taken shape around these two scars.

My instinct is to find something that will either numb the ache, distract me from it or replace it with a positive feeling. That's what I should do right? After all, I should NOT feel sad on a beautiful autumn day when nothing is apparently wrong in my life.

I am very blessed, but I still feel sad.

We feel angry and fearful and annoyed and exhausted and insecure and depressed and a whole host of other things on beautiful autumn days when nothing is apparently wrong in our lives. We feel these things because our life experience carries with it a myriad of longings and memories and wounds and choices and beliefs and nuances.

Like partners on a dance floor, struggle and Blessing move and flow throughout our day.

You are allowed to experience struggle and also welcome Blessing. At times one leads and a few moments later the other steps forward. You don't have to exorcise the one in order to welcome the other. In fact, the awareness of both life's joys and sorrows is a vital part of embracing a balanced human life.

When I allow myself to accept my sadness, my loneliness AND Blessing, I see my day as beautiful choreography:

Sadness AND ... the blessing of rest

Loneliness AND ... the blessing of a nourishing breakfast

Sadness AND ... the blessing of unhurried time

Loneliness AND ... the blessing of the sun's warmth on my skin

Sadness AND ... the blessing of movement and vigor as I walked

Loneliness AND ... the blessing of communication from loved ones.

Sadness AND ... the blessing of sending messages of love to others.

Loneliness AND ... the blessing of pouring out my thoughts in my journal

Sadness AND ... the blessing of reading inspiring words of others on the journey

Loneliness AND ... the blessing of smelling and tasting hearty food

Yes, I felt sad and lonely throughout the day, but I also hung a dozen or more beautiful pictures on the cracked walls of my sacred space. As I did, the ache lessened and the goodness could seep in.

> ### Blessing provides a beautiful and intentional way to move through struggles toward the things you desire.

When trauma, heartache, illness or serious struggle enter our lives, Blessing is not a magic wand that wipes it all away. It does, however, empower you to not be a victim to your circumstances. My life experiences may have wired me to default toward a particular set of emotions, but each moment offers me the opportunity to make a different choice. I choose the truth that sadness and loneliness may be PART of my story, but they are not the whole story. They carry echoes of my true home where I once experienced pure joy and complete belonging.

Today, I invited Blessing to enter the places that hurt. I allowed myself to consider a different possibility. To think a different thought. To believe a different truth. It went something like this:

You are not alone. All over the world are people, just like you, who are making their way through this day. Feeling a little off. Feeling a little low. Feeling like they aren't quite living their best life. They, too, feel the ache. And it's ok. Not every day has to be amazing or epic or productive or even happy. It's ok to allow and to even embrace the simple magic of an ordinary, good-enough day. And this ache? This ache is not meant to be cured. It is meant to return you, again and again and again to Source. To Love. It is meant to keep you homesick for your true home so that you won't forget. So ease up on yourself and allow this day to be good – even with its moments that are hard. Breathe in the abundance of goodness that surrounds you. Even when your heart aches, all is well. Know that you are never out of Love's reach.

Rather than ignoring, resisting or wallowing in your dominant, encoded emotions, simply accept that they represent part of your current human journey. They are not a life sentence and their existence does disqualify you from appreciating the good and beautiful things in your life. Pain and joy can co-exist.

Lifelong patterns take time to change. Give yourself loving permission to allow struggle and Blessing to co-exist in your life. The more beautiful pictures you hang on your walls, the less you'll notice the cracks and peeling paint. Every time you choose to introduce a new element into the Petri-dish of your life, everything shifts a little.

Every choice either weakens or strengthens your being.

You get to decide.

I've been on this Blessing journey for a few years now and there is no doubt that the biological, chemical, emotional set-point for my life has changed. I feel stronger and more hopeful. I feel more balanced and at peace. Even on the hard days, I am aware of goodness and light. Slowly, my brain, my body and my spirit are aligning with truth.

Dear reader, you and I are allowed to be happy even if our hearts still ache under the smiles. We are allowed to weave strands of peace throughout our worry. We are allowed to rest even though our to-do lists aren't finished. We are allowed to enjoy moments of connection even if we feel lonely again almost immediately. We are allowed to feel joy in the midst of sadness.

We are allowed to thrive while we continue to heal.

We are allowed to decorate all of the walls of our crazy, messy, imperfect lives with blessings and call them beautiful. THAT is the power of Blessing!

Blessing As a Lifestyle

When I think back to my childhood in rural Ohio, very few monumental memories rise to the surface. Other than a few vacations and typical family milestones, the majority of my memories center around little day-to-day happenings. Moments so ordinary that my parents probably never knew I noticed them. I'm sure they didn't imagine I would be smiling fondly at these snapshots of life 40 years later.

I remember the smell of my father's hair grease, the way he carefully sliced a half banana onto his bowl of Wheaties each morning, the snapping sound as he latched the tabs on his grey metal lunchbox. Thinking of my mother brings another set of precious memories – her beautiful soprano voice wafting through the house as she worked, the peach iced tea she drank every afternoon at 4pm, the way she slicked down my fly-away hairs as if they were sin itself, the clack-clack of her typewriter behind the closed door of the den.

I can still hear the slam of the wooden screen door, smell the meatloaf baking every Sunday afternoon, see the graceful billow of the long white curtain in the hallway as the breeze wafted through the window. Cool dewy grass under my bare feet returns me to Ohio evenings where the fireflies waltzed over the darkening lawn to the backdrop of the nightly baseball game on the radio.

Writing from the perspective of an adult, I realize how each of these sights, smells, sounds and memories shaped my life. My parents were creatures of habit. Good habits. Even to this day, my eight-eight-year-old dad combs his hair with the same grease and methodically slices a half banana onto his Wheaties every morning!

Our simple life would be considered utterly boring by today's standards, but it was completely stable and predictable. Every day at 3:15 pm, Dad's car pulled in the driveway and dinner was on the table by 5pm. Every Wednesday night, we attended church. On Thursday nights, we popped popcorn and played board games. Saturday nights, we enjoyed pizza and our once-a-week bottle of Dr. Pepper. If the Cleveland Indians were playing on the east coast, my brother and I were allowed to stay up late to listen to the end of the game. Sunday morning was church again, meatloaf and baked potatoes for lunch and afternoon naps followed by a family walk.

Without words, these routines provided the foundation of security and care upon which my early life was built. Of reserved German ancestry, my mother and father never gushed about how proud they were of me or how much they loved me. But the rock-solid consistency of their lifestyle resonated deep within my tiny body, shaping my thoughts, emotions and world view. Day after day after day. Using a thousand unspoken blessings, my parents created a home where I could flourish.

Too often, we live our lives in search of the grand moments when everything aligns. We think that a job promotion, a flashy vacation, finding our soul mate, having a baby, buying a dream house, seeing our child accepted to the right college and finally enjoying a comfortable retirement will prove that we've been blessed. These milestone events dangle before us with the glitter of diamonds. Precious, sparkling and rare enough that we can only hope to collect a few over an entire lifetime.

In between the flashy diamond moments, lie thousands of ordinary days.

Like pearls forming through the daily grind of sand and sea, our lives take shape during the "day after day after day-ness" of life. Have you ever considered the routines you have already settled into? Routines that impact not only your life but the lives of those who share time and space with you. You wake. You sleep. You come.

You go. You work. You play. You eat. You drink. You do it all again tomorrow.

Through these routines, you create your life. This life is not a dress rehearsal. Are you intentionally shaping a life you love? Or are you simply going through motions of reacting and surviving?

Blessing makes a perfect companion for real, raw, wonderful, messy, beautiful, scary, happening-faster-than-you-can-keep-up LIFE. You don't need elaborate meditations, prayers, ceremonies or rituals. Anyone can bless anything at any moment of any day. Short and sweet. Blessing can be whispered under the breath, sent across miles through a thought, delivered through a hand on the shoulder or served on a paper plate disguised as a reheated leftover dinner.

The secret is intention: Blessing on purpose.

On hot summer days, I love to use my infusion pitcher. In the center is a slotted tube that I fill with creative combinations like cucumber/mint, lemon/blueberry, strawberry/basil. Then I add water. Plain water. As I go about my day, the fruity flavors from the central tube seep into the pitcher and transform that ordinary water into a refreshing treat worthy of "ooohs and ahhhs."

In the same way, when the intention of blessing seeps from the center of your heart into the ordinary moments of your day, it infuses everything and everyone around you. Every single action you perform becomes special. Simple moments suddenly matter. The way you spend your waking moments, prepare for the day, react to a rude driver, perform your tasks, listen to your friend, feed your body, fold the laundry, help with homework, talk with your spouse, hug your child good night, unwind and settle into bed … these are the plain water moments of your day that await the infusion of Blessing.

Ancient people understood the infusion of Blessing into daily life. From sunup to sundown, they blessed their way through the day. When they pressed a seed into the soil, they blessed the future crop. When they harvested the grain, they blessed the earth that caused it to grow. When they formed a loaf of bread, they blessed the fire that baked it. When they gathered around the table, they blessed the loved ones and the stranger who joined them. They blessed the rain that filled their wells. They blessed the days, the months, the seasons. They blessed those embarking on a journey and blessed their joyous returning. They blessed warriors charging into battle. They blessed sailors tossed at sea. They blessed hunters seeking food. They blessed their children and their children's children. They blessed the aged and the dying.

What a beautiful way to live!

You deserve to live immersed in Blessing as well! While it may feel a little odd to bless your coffee pot, your laptop, your water faucet, the produce manager at the supermarket, your boss, the Uber driver or your child's soccer team, these are the modern-day equivalents to the way our ancestors covered their days in Blessing.

> ### From morning to night,
> ### you encounter thousands of
> ### moments in which you can
> ### weave the power and mystery
> ### of Blessing into your daily life.

Try it. Practice it. You will feel strange at first. Maybe you'll only remember a few times a day. Setting a timer on your phone can help. The words may come slowly at first, but remember, you can't mess up a blessing!

Whether spoken or unspoken, be assured that any blessing you invite is already on its way. Even if you don't see an immediate change, keep blessing. The current atmosphere of your home didn't take shape overnight and it will take time to shift deeply ingrained patterns. Remember that change begins first in the unseen world of thought, emotion, energy and vibration.

The invisible world shapes the visible one – both scientifically and spiritually.

To the Next Generation

My grandparents raised eleven children during the Great Depression and both World Wars. Like most families of that era, the struggle to feed and clothe all those children consumed their time and energy. There were no leisurely play dates at the local park, family vacations or even the luxury of school sports. Until he passed away at age 91, my grandfather's life revolved around hard work, faith and family. He left a simple legacy: one small farm and nine surviving children.

Recently, my father and his siblings, now in their 70's and 80's gathered for a reunion. As usual, the conversation eventually flowed to reminiscing about their childhood days. All went well until one of my uncles chuckled and said, "I've never brought this up before, but I always knew I was Dad's favorite."

"Oh no you weren't!" a chorus of protests erupted.

"I was the hands-down favorite," an aunt insisted.

"No ... I always felt sorry for the rest of you because I was Dad's favorite."

For the next hour, stories flew fast and furious as each sibling offered rock-solid proof to back up their claim. Incredibly, they realized that each of them had carried a secret, lifelong certainty that they were "dad's favorite." Long before today's wealth of child-rearing books, podcasts or parenting blogs, my quiet, hard-working grandfather managed to make every one of his children believe that they held a uniquely special place in his heart. What a legacy!

Sadly, not everyone shares this experience. Some children grow up surrounded by negativity, stress, demeaning remarks and various forms of abuse. Even in loving homes, well-meaning parents make careless comments, get too caught up in work and life's stress and unintentionally miss opportunities to delight in their children. I've sat with children, teens, young adults, middle-aged men and old women as they've remembered the moments that shaped their lives. Here are just a few of the things they've told me:

"My dad always pinched my waist and made a "chubby bunny" face if I took a second helping of food."

"My mom works two jobs so she can buy me all the latest clothes and electronics. I just want to spend time with her rather than have all that stuff." (this was a teenager!)

"I played high school basketball for four years, but my dad only made it two of my games."

"My mom is coming to visit and I'm nervous! I may be 66 years old, but she still makes me feel like a stupid kid."

"My dad never calls or visits, but he promised to leave his watch collection to me when he dies. I guess that's the only time of his I'll ever get."

"My dad never told me I was beautiful – not once."

"Everything I do is to make my dad proud of me. But I still don't think he is."

"I don't remember ever hearing my mom say the words I love you."

"I wasn't athletic at all and I always felt my parents' disappointment."

"My dad wanted a boy and here I was, another girl."

"My parents were never happy unless I had straight A's."

"I couldn't wait to show my dad my first home. Instead of congratulating me, he pointed out everything that needed to be fixed."

Pain reverberates through each word. Often the words that haunt us most are the words left unspoken. The words we longed to hear. Many adults live with a deep sense that they were never good enough, smart enough, pretty enough or worthy enough to receive their parents' acceptance or blessing.

We spend our lives working to build financial wealth, buy a family home, create a successful business, give our children the best life, travel to amazing places and hopefully retire comfortably. These are all tangible signs that we've created a good life for ourselves and our children. How often do we ponder the spiritual and emotional legacy we will leave to the generations that follow?

At this point, I can almost hear you groan. *Work pressure, deadlines, bills due, doctor appointments, soccer games, dinner to make…. and you want me to leave behind a great legacy too?*

Yes! But your legacy won't be some grand gesture or an extra item on your daily list.

> ## What your children will remember most is the way you showed love in the simple moments of your daily life.

After years of heartbreak and struggle, I am deeply grateful for the love of my children who are now scattered across the country. My phone buzzes all day long as they share stories of college adventures, work projects, daily stresses and the antics of my beautiful grandchildren. While it seems that our family's story will have a happy ending, I clearly remember that young mother hiding on a pile of dirty laundry so many years ago.

A deep sense of failure saturated every cell of her being. She knew that she wasn't equipped to meet her children's needs. She felt their frustration and feared that they would grow up to hate her. (Miraculously, they didn't!) Looking back with the wisdom and perspective of years, I see now that even though she made a lot of mistakes, she also did a lot of things right. She loved her children hard and strong. And so do you.

Parenting is a marathon of 9,460,800 moments from birth to your child's 18th birthday. Before you cross the finish line (which is really the beginning of a whole new race), you'll do a few million things that seem unnoticed and unappreciated. You'll perform mundane tasks over and over and over while wishing you could do something more meaningful. You'll lay awake at night filled with worry and self-doubt. You will yell things you don't mean. You will forget things you should have remembered. You will fight inner battles that your children will never understand. Sometimes you will feel like parent-of-the-year and within minutes, you'll imagine your child confiding your failures to a therapist in about 30 years.

Through it all, remember that you are a blessing with skin on! A living, breathing, speaking, hugging, dinner cooking, carpool driving, homework helping, laundry folding, tear wiping, tough love giving, heartbreak consoling, always-trying-to-get-it-right gift to your child. For the few million mistakes you'll make, you'll do even more millions of things well!

Not every moment will be beautiful, but as in any marathon, it's the entire race that counts.

"Not all of us can do great things. But we can do small things with great love." I love these wise words from Mother Theresa, a woman who never had biological children but who mothered many. My grandfather certainly embodied this truth with his quiet life of faithful moments.

From tying their shoes to chewing with their mouths closed, from dribbling a basketball to being kind to others, you will teach your children many important lessons. But they will also learn things you've never consciously taught them. You'll hear your words coming out of their mouths or see them mimic something you do. Much of your legacy will be "caught not taught" as they absorb many qualities and values simply from observing the way you engage in life. Let this be your motivation to do your own inner work and show them the path to managing difficult moments and emotions.

Every day provides countless opportunities to answer the soul questions your children's hearts are asking.

Do I belong?
Am I safe?
Does my story matter?

Remember the Cleansing and then Blessing model. Don't just clean up your act, but intentionally fill your child's heart and home with words and actions of Blessing. Affirm daily how much you love them and how proud they make you. Be sure to bless them not only when they do well, but also just because they exist. Don't assume that they know how much you care. Make sure they do!

Can children learn to bless themselves? Yes! Even the youngest child can learn to speak healthy words into their atmosphere. Build a simple Blessing practice into your daily schedule through moments when you're already connecting. Early morning cuddles can be a time to speak blessings or teach your child simple affirmations. A quick blessing as they head out for the school bus sets the tone for the entire day. A fist bump or special handshake gives them the blessing of your support as they head out on the soccer field. Mealtimes, homework time and especially bedtime are great times to bless.

Within your home, your child's bedroom is his or her sacred space. If your children share a bedroom, be sure that each child has a space to claim as their own. Help them create a safe haven by choosing special items that focus on the blessings they want or need. Decorate their room with items that celebrate joy or courage or friendship. Rather than banishing them to their room as a punishment, show them how to use time in their room as a "reset" button.

Teach your child to listen to the messes in his emotional messes and to choose a blessing that will shift his thoughts and emotions to a more positive place. Any of the blessings in the back of this book can be adapted for children. Using simple terms, you can talk about erasing or wiping away angry or sad thoughts. Even a small child can understand choosing kind and happy thoughts. Some of the best blessings for children are the 10-Second blessing, the Flip It blessing or the Breath In/Breath Out blessing. An older child can write down what's bothering her, tear up the paper and then write a blessing in its place.

By evening, we parents are exhausted and ready to be done with the day. Your day may have had its share of mad dashes, frustrated yelling and other less than stellar parental moments. You may be tempted to rush the kids off to bed so you can finally relax, but the way you end the day matters. Taking time to bless your child can erase a lot of the day's damage. Many families use bedtime for extra cuddles and prayers.

Create simple Blessing routines that your child looks forward to. One of my daughters loved it when I kissed the palm of her hand each night. She curled her chubby fingers around the invisible kiss to hold it all night long. Sometimes she would "drop" the kiss and call me back into the room to give her another one. Make it your goal to send your child off to dreamland with a sense of deep love and security.

Of all the things you do in life, the nurturing of your children will be your greatest life work. Blessing your home will create a far greater ripple effect than getting them into the best schools, dressing them in top brands or buying the latest electronic gadget. What happens in your home creates the set point for their lives and the resulting patterns will impact future generations.

So bless and bless and bless some more! You'll never be regret a single moment spent in blessing your children. Let Blessing be your legacy!

Beyond Your Home

Home lies at the deepest part of our human need. When we truly feel at home, we know that we belong, that we are safe and that our story matters. If this book guides you to create a lovely home for your body and spirit, my heart will be full of gratitude.

However, there is more. As living in a blessed home becomes your new "normal," a strange and powerful thing will occur. Your heart will expand and your eyes will open to see that you are part of a much larger home. Beyond the walls where you eat and sleep lies another home. A home found in the streets of your community, the landscapes of your country and in a beautiful family of brothers and sisters around the world.

As the sacred space of your home begins to heal, you will become more aware of the negative attitudes, harmful behaviors and toxic energies that surround you. Suddenly your coworker's rants about your boss won't feel so harmless. You'll cringe when you hear a friend speaking harshly about her body. News headlines of tragedy and turmoil will raise your awareness of how many people feel angry, frightened and hopeless.

From politics to protests to promoting awareness, our culture seems obsessed with all that is wrong in the world. Your old, familiar reaction may be to join the vast vibration of stress, anger and hand-wringing. It can feel like your civic duty to throw yourself into the fight – posting passionately on social media, rallying against injustice, walking in a 5K for cancer prevention or baking brownies for the animal shelter fundraiser. All good things, right?

But remember that what we focus on grows. What we speak becomes.

In our zeal to make a difference, we often contribute to the strengthening of the very ideas, emotions and vibrations we wish to change. A perfect example has been the presidency of Donald Trump. With friends in both political parties, I have a front-row seat to very passionate opinions. Normally kind and loving people openly and proudly declare their pure hatred of President Trump. Because they feel that his policies promote hatred, they hate him with a passion! On the other side, those who support President Trump feel frustrated and offended and begin to hate those speaking against him. Over the past few years, I've seen friends part ways and families torn apart by their disagreements over this man. Rather than promoting peace or love, the intense focus on hatred stirs up more dissension and distrust. There are many who fear it will tear our country apart. As my mother used to tell me, "Two wrongs don't make a right!"

In order to change the world, we must move from fighting AGAINST what is wrong to working FOR what is right. Just that simple shift in thinking makes a tremendous difference in how you bring healing and compassion into a hurting world. We must acknowledge the wrongs, but give our passion and energy to creating the world we wish to live in.

> ## What happens in homes around the world matters more than what takes place in any corporate boardroom, newsroom or even the White House.

Through the seemingly private, hidden act of blessing your home, you release healing and transformation that ripples far beyond your four walls. When you see the entire world as your home, you realize that you can apply the same principles of Cleansing and Blessing to create a blessed home on a larger scale – a blessed world!

Instead of contributing to the negativity, pain, fear or outrage, you can shift the conversation. You can be the hand that reaches across the economic, social, racial or religious divide to help another.

You can be the voice that says, "We are all in this together. Let's figure it out." You can intentionally bring Blessing into your neighborhood, your school, your workplace, your church (yes, they need blessing too!) and your circle of friends.

Now more than ever, humanity longs to know the answers to their soul questions.

Do I belong?

Am I safe?

Does my story matter?

Just as the messes in your home carry messages, so do the larger messes of our world! Listen to the messages and be a channel to invite Blessing from the spiritual world to the physical one. When you sit in the carpool line, bless the frazzled mom with smeared mascara and a messy bun. At work, bless the coworker muttering under his breath. As you walk your dog, bless each home you pass. When you hear bad news, bless the people suffering from tragedy, disease or poverty. When you hear a siren, bless the ones in trouble and the courageous firefighters and paramedics rushing to the scene. When your friend complains about her spouse, bless their marriage. At the school concert or sporting event, bless each child and family. When you pass a hospital, bless the sick with health. When you pass a jail, bless the prisoners with true mental and emotional freedom.

When I began writing this book, I held the vision of thousands of people creating homes where Blessing flows through their daily routine as naturally as breathing, sleeping or eating. Now as I finish the book, my vision has expanded to seeing healing light from those blessed homes spilling out into the streets, shining across communities, countries and continents. This may seem like a crazy big dream for a tiny little book, but every world-changing movement begins with a single thought.

Think of me as you bless your home. I will think of you.

Moment by moment. Choice by choice. Home by home. Together, may we create homes for our spirits, havens for our loved ones and beautiful healing in our world.

May the sun bring you
energy by day,
May the moon softly
restore you by night,

May the breeze blow new
strength into your being.

May you walk gently
through the world
And know its beauty all
the days of your life.

APACHE BLESSING

PART 4

Blessing Guide

During some seasons of life, our days are a whirl of activity, expectations and demands. Everyone else comes first leaving us with only a few moments (or seconds!) a day to think about our own needs. Other seasons allow us to live at a slower pace where we can devote intentional time to creating a practice of self-care and blessing. No matter which stage you're in, each word or act of Blessing brings the beautiful essence of your spirit's home into your physical home.

Allow your personality, your lifestyle and your core values to guide you just as you do when decorating your physical home. In the following section, you will find:

- simple blessings for the days when you need to bless on the run
- specific situation blessings
- room-by-room blessings to create a sanctuary in every room of your home.

You don't have to use all of these blessings. Pick the ones that resonate with you. Feel free to adapt them to fit your home's needs. In time, you'll develop your own blessings as you create a sacred space where your spirit truly feels at home.

Simple Blessings

The alarm didn't go off. Coffee sloshes down the front of your new blouse. Traffic makes you late for an important meeting. The school calls about your son's attitude. Your dinner burns. We've all had days when everything goes wrong and our mood heads downhill fast. Time for a quick Blessing fix!

The blessings in this section only take a few seconds - perfect for busy days. Each one is based on an analogy designed to stick easily in your mind. Choose two or three of your favorites and think of them as tools in your toolbox to help you reset your home's atmosphere on the run!

10 Second Blessing Blast

Do a quick "scan" of your home. What is the first thing you notice or feel? What are the attitudes, words and body language of yourself or the others in your home? What energy dominates at the moment?

Perhaps everyone seems exhausted. Because this is a quick blessing blast, you don't need to figure out the cause of the exhaustion right now. You're going to use the power of your spoken word to invite the OPPOSITE to flow through your home.

Stand still right in the middle of it all and take a deep breath in and out. Speak the blessing that you most would like your family to experience instead of exhaustion. "Let there be ENERGY for the work we must do." "Let there be RELAXATION and PEACE." "Let there be inner CALM in this home tonight."

For 10 seconds, speak as many blessings as come to your mind – rapid-fire - then simply move on with your day. No need to focus on the issue anymore unless you want. Perhaps a few hours later, you see another area where your home needs to be blessed. Because the 10 Second Blessing Blast is so short, you can use it dozens of times a day.

"Stronger Than" Blessing

At some point, almost every kid brags "my dad is stronger than your dad" or "you do that again and my brother will beat you up after school." Hopefully as adults, we no longer need to call in our dad or brother to handle our problems. But even in the safety of our own homes, we can feel bullied by the stresses and pressures of life. We need a strategy to stand up in courage and confidence. This blessing does just that! In fact, it even brags a little!

The formula is simple: "My _____ is stronger than this _____."

Here are some examples:

My joy is stronger than this sadness.

My hope is stronger than this depression.

My connection to loving people is stronger than this loneliness.

My peace is stronger than this anxiety.

At first, you may feel foolish speaking things that don't seem true. It's hard to believe in the strength of joy when tears of frustration flow. Remember that you don't have to create or manufacture the blessing. The joy you desire already exists as a powerful force in the world. Use your spoken words to connect with your spirit's home where all blessings flow.

Place the Order Blessing

Once considered mysterious and even dangerous, online shopping is now the preferred method of buying for many people. No longer must you drive from store to store and deal with salesmen and showrooms. In the comfort of your home, you browse through more choices than imaginable just a few years ago, load items into your virtual shopping cart and joyfully press the "Place Order" button. From that moment on, you consider these items to be yours, counting the days until they arrive.

Even though you've only seen a photo, you announce, "My new couch is coming on Thursday!" You haven't sat on this couch for even a minute. For all you know, it could be lying in pieces in a factory somewhere, but you are not concerned in the least. You have full confidence that your new couch is on the way and that it is better than the old couch you're sending to the curb.

In the same way, you can be sure that the blessings you invite are on their way. Consciously "place the order" for what you want and begin to speak of it as already yours. *"I am excited about the close friendships I am building." "I give thanks for the amazing health and energy I enjoy." "I can't wait to feel peace instead of this anxiety."*

Your stronger, more beautiful life is on the way – even before you can see it!

Cancel the Order Blessing

Have you ever placed an online order only to realize seconds later that you purchased the wrong size or color? If you move quickly enough, you can go into your order history and cancel the thing you just ordered. Wouldn't it be great if you had a "Cancel" button for negativity? You do!

Your words can order either blessing or more stress and struggle. When you catch yourself in the middle of a negative spiral, stop and say the word "CANCEL" out loud as a way to interrupting the words or thoughts that you were just spewing. You don't want more financial stress, cranky kids or piles of laundry. So cancel that order!

Now speak a blessing to replace the words you were just saying. For example, if you were just complaining about how "I can never get ahead financially," CANCEL. Now speak what you DO want. "I bless my life with abundance and financial wisdom."

Breathe In/Breath Out Blessing

Breathing is not optional! No matter how busy our day, we breathe thousands of times a day. Our bodies do their job with or without our conscious thought, but bringing awareness to your breath provides a great opportunity to choose a deeper purpose. In recent years, breathwork has been recognized as a tool to calm, center, restore and heal both mind and body.

Since you have to breathe anyway, choose to use a few of your daily breaths and make them conscious acts of Blessing. When you feel stressed, angry or anxious, take a few slow, deep breaths. What negativity do you want to release?

Breathe out the negativity you don't want.
Breathe in the blessing you want.
Breathe out stress.
Breathe in peace.
Breathe out fear.
Breath in courage.

As you breathe in, envision sending the blessing to any part of your body that feels tense or distressed. Many people find that inhaling and exhaling with purpose during a workout, a jog/walk or during yoga connects the body and spirit in a meaningful way. Because breathing is an unspoken blessing, you can practice it anywhere – in a stressful meeting, in the few seconds before you lose it with your kids, while waiting at a traffic light or in bed before you fall asleep.

Flip the Coin Blessing

Everything has an opposite. Hot vs. Cold. Dark vs. Light. Soft vs. Hard. Sweet vs Bitter. Fast vs. Slow. You get the idea! Emotions have opposites too. Take a moment to tune in to what you're feeling. Lonely? Overwhelmed? Disappointed? Annoyed?

Once you identify the emotion, imagine that it is one side of a coin and the other side represents the opposite emotion. Picture yourself flipping that coin over in the palm of your hand. As you do, say, "I exchange this loneliness for the blessing of connection." or "I exchange being overwhelmed for the blessing of calmness and order."

You may be tempted to think this is too simple or too cheesy to work. Just remember that you get to choose and design your environment. As you walk about in the "petri dish" of your body, you can introduce a new element any time you wish. Every single thought either weakens or strengthens your cells. Every time you "flip the coin," you inject a little more joy, peace or love into your body's petri dish. So flip away!

Flavor of the Day Blessing

Near our home is a legendary ice cream stand that makes exactly one flavor a day. You might find yourself standing in line for peanut butter ice cream. Or black raspberry. Or peach. Or peppermint. Although other ice cream shops in the area offer twenty or more flavors, people drive from miles around to get their hands on the flavor of the day. Since the ice cream gurus only make one kind of ice cream a day, they spare no effort in making it the BEST flavor. One lick and the flavor almost bursts in your mouth.

If figuring out multiple blessings for your home and family members feels overwhelming, choose a flavor of the day. First thing in the morning, decide what blessing you need most. Will it be joy? Hope? Safety? Courage? Patience? As you go through your day, bless everything and everyone with your one chosen blessing.

Remember that one flavor doesn't mean boring or ineffective. One can mean the BEST. The focus and intention of your blessing may be more powerful because you are pouring all of your Blessing "guru-ness" into that one area.

Lifestyle Blessings

Blessing once held a place of honor in the daily routines of many civilizations. The lines between the physical and spiritual worlds were not so clearly defined and our ancestors believed in the power of blessing. While some cultures held elaborate ceremonies to mark special occasions, most blessings were simply woven into the daily rhythm of working, eating and sleeping.

While writing elaborate blessings and holding ceremonies is meaningful, don't make Blessing harder than it has to be! Making Blessing a natural part of your daily routine will yield much more consistent and effective results. Here are some of the key times of the day that can serve as natural reminders to bless:

- waking moments
- first sip of coffee
- putting the kids on the bus/dropping them off at school
- clocking in at work
- lunch break
- workout/walking the dog
- commute (what better way to spend time stuck in traffic!)
- returning home
- mealtimes
- evening shower
- bedtime

Because you repeat these moments day after day after day, they provide the perfect system for infusing meaning and blessing into your daily life. You're going to do them anyway, so make them count. Choose two or three key routines and make them a focal point for intentional blessing.

Here are some blessings for your daily routine.

Morning Blessing

How do you begin your day? With a beeping alarm? A crying child? Your dog licking your face? Perhaps you have the luxury of stretching and waking slowly as your eyes flicker with the first glimmer of morning light. As you reach full awareness, what thoughts fill your mind? What is the first act of your day?

I'm ashamed to admit that all too often, the first act of my day involves scrolling through a social media news feed, mindlessly absorbing the endless stream of cute kids, crazy animal pranks and political rants. Or I begin mulling over my never-ending list of worries: the bill that's due, the child who is struggling, the friend who seems to be growing distant.

We all know better and yet we choose to shove the virtual equivalent of a fistful of junk food into our emotional mouths before we've even rolled out of bed.

Our early waking moments are the purest and most potential-filled of our day. Before the noise and stress of the world crowds in, we hold a small precious window of time that is all ours. (Mothers of young children, I see you. You will have to tweak this concept a bit for your stage of life.) What we do in those first moments holds more power than we can imagine.

Most spiritual traditions and inspirational teachers encourage a morning routine of worship, reading, gratitude, self-care and prayer. As a child, I was taught to have daily devotional time. Unfortunately, I viewed this more as a duty than a blessing. Motivated by earning points in Sunday School, I faithfully said my prayers and checked off chapters on my Bible reading chart. Many years later, I willingly returned to these practices as a way to connect with God, receive guidance and align my mind and heart with what really matters. Mornings set the tone not only for the day ahead, but ultimately for my life.

In his best-selling book, the Miracle Morning, Hal Elrod reminds us that "how you do anything is how you do everything."[18] We may think that each individual little choice doesn't matter, but over time, those seemingly harmless "in the moment" choices become habits. Beginning with the first choice of each day, we systematically create the person we are becoming and the life we will live.

Because living a life of beauty and purpose is one of my core values, I've begun to hold the world at bay for just a few moments when I wake. As I roll over and stretch, my first words are now a whispered "thank you." I refuse to allow myself to pick up my phone until I've intentionally invited joy and beauty into my thoughts. My waking moments are now a cherished time of connection to my spirit's home while my day is still untainted.

There is no better way to begin creating a blessed home than by choosing Blessing as the first conscious act of each day!

"As morning light pushes back the darkness of night, I give thanks for the shelter and safety in which I've rested. May the rising sun spread its promise over my home and may its rays warm any cold or dark places within me. May I breathe in the fresh air of this morning with hope and anticipation, knowing that new possibility, new adventure and new mercy is given to me. Not only is this morning a fresh start, but I can begin again as many times as I need throughout the day. May I face the challenges of this day with courage and creativity. May I bless my body and spirit with the nourishment of beauty, good food, movement, laughter and moments where I notice and embrace life's simple joys. May I remember that each person I meet has a story and may I have the wisdom and compassion to listen – whether they tell that story through words or actions. May my words be empowering and kind – especially the ones I speak to myself. May I do my day's tasks with purpose and passion, as if my work could change the world - because it does. May I brighten someone's day. May I create something that makes me smile. May I take one more step toward living the dreams in my heart. Most of all, as the sun sets this evening, may I feel satisfied that I have done the best I could to live and love well on this precious day."

Leaving and Entering Blessing

When you leave your home, you step from your haven into the outside world. It may sound silly, but the way you enter that world matters. You can scurry out the door with your mind whirling, arms loaded, yelling at the kids to hurry up and already dreading the traffic, the appointments, the annoyances. Or you can enter the world with grace and hope - taking just a moment to bless the people and events that lie ahead.

Similarly, when you re-enter your home, you can drag in the door in a frazzled state, exhausted and agitated. Or you can pause for a moment and make the choice to leave the day's stresses outside. After all, do you really want to bring the snarky coworker, the impatient driver and the tantruming toddler home with you? (Well ... I guess you have to bring home the toddler if it belongs to you!)

These ordinary moments, repeated thousands of times in our lifetime, represent two powerful transition points in your day. Simply being aware of crossing the threshold adds a different perspective to your life.

Upon leaving your home – pause for a moment inside your door and bless:

"I enter the world with love. May I be safe. May I be wise. May I be kind. May I be divinely guided. May I be a blessing to all"

Upon entering your home – pause for a moment outside your door and bless:

"I enter my home with love. May I be safe. May I be wise. May I be kind. May I be divinely guided. May I be a blessing to all"

Note: These blessings can be especially meaningful when sending children to school or welcoming them home. Many children struggle with classwork, stress, and social anxiety that they may not even be able to express. Practicing a simple ritual to reset their mind before and after school can be very empowering for them.

People I Love Blessing

After years of wanting a gallery wall, I finally rolled up my sleeves last summer and gathered photos of our parents, children and grandchildren. After printing photos of all sizes and purchasing an assortment of coordinating frames, I spent an entire afternoon arranging and rearranging until every photo had found its spot. The result: one entire wall of my family room decorated with the faces of the people I love.

As I've grown deeper into the practice of Blessing as a lifestyle, this "wall of love" has become the perfect visual reminder to bless the people I love. Sometimes I'll just stand and look at it for a few moments, mentally sending loving thoughts to each person. Other times, as I pass by, I'll whisper a blessing to one person who I sense needs an extra boost that day.

If you don't have the space to create an entire wall of photos, gather your photos into a small album. You can also create a special folder on your phone with digital photos of your friends and family. Seeing everyone's face in the same place makes it simple to spend a few moments a day consciously sending blessings their way.

One of my friends wrote a personalized blessing for each family member and she reads them several times a week. This is a beautiful way to capture all of your wishes for that person and bless any areas where they may be struggling. If you don't have the time to do that, you can bless them with whatever you feel they need that day. My favorite way to bless my loved ones is simple but powerful.

"May you be safe. May you be happy. May you be strong. May you be at peace."

Mealtime Blessing

Even if you did not grow up in a faith-based home, you've probably experienced the tradition of blessing the food or "saying grace" before a meal. At least three times a day, most of us take time to eat. These already established routines provide the perfect opportunity to add gratitude, mindfulness and blessing to your day.

During a visit to a retreat center, each morning began with silent breakfast. Several hundred people filled the tables with not a sound other than the occasional clink of silverware. As we nourished our bodies, we were encouraged to focus on gratitude and I realized how powerful these few moments could be. I actually tasted my food, felt gratitude for the farmers and bakers who created it and pondered the day ahead.

Pause as you take your first sip of morning coffee. Savor the first hot bite of your evening meal. These simple steps will calm you, bring a centering peace to your body and may even help with the digestion process. Those who study energy tell us that gratitude is one of the highest vibrations so choosing to be grateful will always shift the atmosphere of your home.

Mealtime blessings and prayers abound so feel free to use one that is meaningful or familiar to you. If you don't have a favorite blessing, here is a simple example:

"I give thanks for this food and I bless the many people who have been part of bringing it to my table. May it nourish and strengthen my body and spirit so that I may bring greater blessing to my world."

Best/Worst Blessing

How often do you ask someone about their day and they reply, "it was good?" Not very helpful! This Blessing routine makes a great debriefing tool at the end of the day. You can do this around the dinner table or use it as a bedtime ritual. If you live alone, you can take a few moments to answer these questions in your journal.

Ask each person two questions:

"What was the best moment of your day?"

"What was the worst moment of your day?"

After each person answers, combine the best and worst parts of their day into a blessing. Suppose your partner shares that the best part of the day was the hilarious antics of his coworker at lunch while the worst part of the day was a looming project deadline. You can combine these two extremes into something like this: *"I bless you with more moments of joy and laughter and with wisdom and energy for the project you're facing."*

By speaking blessing to the positive moment of the day, you are strengthening that vibration even more. Your loved one will relive that happy moment and feel a surge of positive emotion just by hearing you invite more of that into his/her life. Also when you speak blessing to the negative moment of the day, you weaken and shift that vibration by inviting something better. Remember the prayer of St. Francis. "Where there is doubt, faith. Where there is despair, hope."

For example, today I really enjoyed a phone conversation with my daughter but also struggled with feeling ignored by another person I care about. I can channel these two extremely different emotions into a blessing: *"I bless my beautiful, deep, and fun relationships with my children and I also bless myself with knowing that I am loved by many. I am worthy of love no matter how another person responds on a given day."*

Body Care Blessing

Our body is our most intimate home, the physical temple that houses our spirit. Although they deserve reverent care, we often treat our bodies with casual indifference that borders on rudeness! We eat junk food, stay up too late, rarely exercise and allow stress to flood our bodies with almost constant surges of disease-causing chemicals. Then when some part of our body breaks down, we feel startled, betrayed and vulnerable.

My personal health journey taught me that our minds, bodies and spirits are intricately connected. Our thoughts and emotions affect our physical health and vice versa. Taking time each day to consciously bless your body can greatly impact how you think and feel about yourself and your overall life. Physically, you can bless your body with nourishing foods, strengthening activities, encouraging relationships and consistent rest. Emotionally, forgiving others, clearing trapped emotions and pursuing your dreams creates a powerful resonance that heals and blesses every cell of your body.

Remember that YOUR voice is the voice that your body listens to the most. As you speak, your brain releases cascades of chemicals and hormones that saturate every organ, gland and bodily process. By choosing to bless yourself, you have the power to literally infuse every cell of your body with kindness and love.

Body image is a struggle for most of us. You may not feel love toward your physical body. Perhaps you dislike its shape, its weight or some part that doesn't function as you wish it would. If you're like most people, you say or think unkind things about your body on a regular basis.

It takes time to reverse the effects of years of negative words and curses you've spoken over yourself. Each word of blessing creates new shifts in your mind and body – allowing your inner and outer self to align into one radiant, beautiful being. I suggest speaking this blessing to yourself when you're alone – perhaps as you awake in the morning or while bathing or grooming. If possible, place your hand on each part of your body as you bless it. (If this blessing does not specify a part of your body that needs special attention, please feel free to add your own blessing for that area of the body.)

I give thanks for my body, my original home on this earth. I appreciate how it has sheltered the true me, carrying me through work and play and sustaining my life - even when I've forgotten, neglected or even misused it. I choose now to honor my body and to bless it. I bless my brain with health and wisdom as it controls my bodily functions and guides my life. May my thoughts be filled with clarity, curiosity and courage. I bless my eyes with clear physical and spiritual vision so that I may see potential, opportunity and beauty in every moment. Knowing that my words are a creative force, may I speak only what is kind, truthful, helpful and inspiring to myself and others. May my heart beat strong and sure as I pursue my daily work and my life's passions. May my lungs expand with cleansing air and the wonder of life itself. May my digestive system efficiently absorb nutrition from the foods I eat and may I release all bodily wastes with ease and comfort. May my arms and legs be strong and flexible for both work and play. May my hands and feet be used to perform good works and increase love on the earth. From head to toe, may my body be blessed. May I be a channel of divine Love. May I open myself to receive the love that flows to me and may I generously release even more love back into the world around me.

Evening Blessing

Just as your morning routine sets the tone for the day, so does ending the day well create a deeper peace for the night that lies ahead. Sleep therapists and experts encourage us to turn off the news, put down our phones, avoid eating, stressful discussions or strenuous activities during our last waking hour. But ending the day with Blessing isn't just about what you stop doing. It is equally important to choose calming, soothing ways to ease yourself toward bedtime. (No … CSI marathons don't count!)

When our girls were young, they had trouble falling asleep – sometimes lying awake until after midnight. Out of sheer desperation, we created an evening routine designed to bring them to a place of peace. After dinner, we let them get their energy out by playing for an hour or so. Then the girls enjoyed warm baths and were slathered with lavender lotion. We lit candles and played beautiful lullaby music while we each rocked or cuddled a wiggly girl. Rubbing their backs and feet also calmed them. Most nights, we were ready to pass out before they were, but this routine established some soothing habits that we still practice most evenings.

How do you spend the last hour of your day? Can you intentionally set aside the business of your day and practice some self-care? Controlling your evening routine can be especially difficult when you have children or share your home with another person. Look for a way to carve out a few moments for yourself. One of my nightly rituals is my bath. Those 20-30 minutes are one of the few uninterrupted times of my day. Not only do I care for my body, but I also reflect on my day and allow my mind to wind down.

Celebrating the high points of the day and releasing the low points through Blessing can help you fall asleep with fewer worries churning through your brain. If you enjoy journaling, bedtime is a great time to write some things you're grateful for or answer the "best/worst" questions suggested earlier. You can also use that time to intentionally bless your family or friends as a final act of love for the day.

"As evening settles over my home, I bless the day that I have just lived. I bless the work that I have done and the work that still remains. May I settle into rest with the knowledge that all is well. I am perfectly aligned with the divine plan for my life. I bless the joyful moments of my day and celebrate the things that made me smile. May I embrace even more joy tomorrow. I bless the moments where I felt connected to another human being – no matter how briefly. May I open my heart even more tomorrow. I bless the strength and health of my body that carried me through this day. May I rise with even greater strength and health tomorrow. I bless the challenges I faced today and the lessons they taught me. May I live with even more courage, compassion and wisdom tomorrow. I bless all those who have cursed me and forgive those who have done evil against me. May I release all hurt, fear, anger and stress and find peace in a fresh start tomorrow. I bless the people I love and this home that shelters me. May we all rest in safety and serenity tonight. May the love in my heart and home shine warmly into the darkness of this night as I surrender to the blessed sleep that will restore my body and spirit."

Special Situation Blessings

Remembering Home Blessing

This method of blessing will take a little more time, but it's time well-spent. When you have 10-15 minutes, find a quiet place, grow still and allow your spirit to connect with your true home.

What do I mean by your true home? As a spiritual being, you were created and brought forth from another place. Your spirit remembers what your mind has long forgotten. Deep within, you remember what it feels like to dwell in perfect love, to never feel alone, to enjoy a sense of peace and safety – all of the things you now desire for your home. The ache and longing that you so often feel (or try to avoid feeling) is actually a remembering, a yearning for the place where you once truly belonged.

As you sit quietly, allow yourself to remember what it feels like to be perfectly at home. Perhaps you will actually picture your childhood home or the home of a friend. Perhaps you will feel frustrated or sad because you never experienced a good home. No matter what your past history, trust that your spirit knows what home feels like.

Allow yourself to breathe in the sense of belonging, comfort, safety, joyfulness, love. See yourself moving through the home, sitting on the chairs, curled up in the bed, laughing around the dinner table, walking barefoot across the lawn. Feeling completely safe and loved.

Spend a few moments connecting to the spiritual memory of home. Feel the emotions of home as deeply as possible. Remember that connecting emotion to new thoughts builds an instant neural synapse. No matter how far from reality this feels, your spirit's home exists and is actually more real and secure than your physical home.

It can never be cluttered or disturbed or destroyed. You are already at home through Blessing, you are going to invite the reality of your true home into your daily physical reality.

When you feel ready to return to your physical home, place your hand over your heart and read the following blessing:

My heart is filled with gratitude for the reality of my spirit's beautiful home. I smile at the memory of this perfect place where I am always welcome, always safe, always loved. When I feel like I don't belong in this world, my spirit can return to its true home at any moment. May the door be opened between the visible and invisible world. May the love, peace and protection of my spiritual home fill the four walls of my physical home. May these sweet memories guide me daily as I care for my earthly home. May God's kingdom come and God's will be done on earth as it is in Heaven.

Crossing the Distance Blessing

Distance between people can exist even within a home. Hectic schedules, exhaustion, endless chores, miscommunication, annoying habits, and financial stresses create emotional and even physical separation between you and your loved ones. You may feel like you live with a bunch of mismatched roommates rather than in a close family. Lying in the dark with a loved one only inches away, one can still feel disconnected and alone.

Blessing brings a powerful awareness that spiritually and energetically, there is no distance. Even when you can't find the words to bridge the gap between you and a loved one, Blessing can cross the divide in a split second. Even a silent blessing acts as a hand reaching over to comfort, connect and raise the other up.

If you sense a distance between you and someone in your home, go to a place where they frequently spend time. Perhaps sit on your child's or in your spouse's favorite chair. If you have a photo of the person, hold it and look "into their face" while you speak this blessing to them.

I am grateful that in sacred space, there is no distance. In this moment, and always, _____ and I are connected emotionally, physically and spiritually. Although our relationship feels difficult and distant at times, I realize that this distance is an illusion created by seeing only with physical eyes and sensing only with surface understanding. In the unseen world, we know and are known. We love and are loved. From this deep place of oneness, I speak Blessing.

Pause for a moment and feel what dominant energy is resonating from your loved one. Is he or she afraid? Overwhelmed? Angry? Lonely? What do you sense he/she needs right now?

I speak the blessing of _____ to (name)_____. No matter how far apart we may feel physically or emotionally, I give thanks that my love can reach him/her. Right now his/her spirit is sensing and receiving this blessing.

May our hearts trust one another's true intentions. May understanding pass between us as we share space in this home. May kindness flow through our thoughts and actions. May grace dance between us – allowing mistakes, learning, growing, forgiving, renewing, embracing – in spirit first, and then in body. May this home be a sheltering place where we feel safe enough to be ourselves, knowing that we will be cherished and accepted. May we find rest as we are both held in Love's strong and gentle hand. I give thanks that all is well.

Special Occasion Blessing

For centuries, Blessing has been an integral part of marking special life occasions. Milestones such as marriage, birth of a child, significant birthdays, graduation, new job or purchase of a home provide the perfect opportunities to focus Blessing toward a loved one.

Do not worry that you're not a great writer, spiritual teacher or theologian. Simply think of the "Catalog of Blessings" (see the Resource section) and ask yourself which two or three blessings seem most needed or appropriate at this time. Thoughtfully write these blessings in a card, or if you are comfortable, actually speak them to the other person.

Many of us spend our whole lives longing to hear Blessing from our parents' lips. Even as adults, we hope to hear words of encouragement from our bosses, our spouses, our friends. Too often, funerals and memorial services are filled with eulogies and tributes containing the very words our loved one has longed to hear. Don't wait to speak words of love and blessing. There is no better time to bless a loved one than when they are crossing a life threshold. You can follow this basic example and add anything else that fits your specific occasion.

On this landmark occasion in your life, I want to acknowledge how special you are in my life. Our relationship brings me joy and I am proud to call you my (friend, sister, child, partner, etc). As you cross this threshold into the next season of life, may you be blessed. I bless you with _____ (blessing) when you face _____ (potential obstacle). May you know _____ (blessing) when you feel _____(possible negative emotion). May your life be filled with an abundance of _____(blessing) when you find yourself_____(possible need). May you know that you are safe. That you belong. That your life matters. And above all else, you are deeply loved!

Walking the Land Blessing

Because the physical and spiritual worlds are inter-connected, walking the perimeter of your home and property carries rich symbolism and spiritual power. As you walk, you physically demonstrate the spiritual reality that you accept your role in guarding, protecting, taking ownership and caring for your space. Even if you are renting, you have the spiritual authority to bless your home. If you are able, walk the entire way around your home or yard and speak the following blessing:

I am honored to be the caretaker for this home. I gratefully accept the responsibility to care for it physically and spiritually. As I walk, I declare blessing with every step. May there be safety within and without these walls. May everyone who enters this space be sheltered in peace. May there be a steady warmth of love and companionship. May this home be filled with an abundance of time together, memories made, lessons learned and grace given. May those who dwell here truly feel at home. May Love's light shine from this home to bring greater joy and healing into the world.

Room-by-Room Blessings

Your home may be a corner of a basement or a penthouse. You may live in three rooms or thirty! No matter the size, each space in your home serves a very clear purpose. Some rooms provide a location for gathering and activity while other rooms nurture rest and self-care. You can invite general blessings into your home, but there is an even greater benefit to blessing each room individually based on its purpose.

Spend a few moments in each room, looking at the space through the eyes of Blessing. Think of the ways your family uses the room – not just physically, but also emotionally and spiritually. Using the "Catalog of Blessings" in the Resource section, choose the blessings you want to emphasize in each room. You can use spoken and unspoken ways of inviting these specific qualities to be part of the atmosphere of the room.

Below are some blessings I've written for the rooms in my home.

Kitchen – If your house is like mine, everyone ends up in the kitchen! While the chaos and mess can be frustrating at times, this room is VITAL to the emotional and physical health of your family. The kitchen literally represents nourishment as we prepare the food that keeps our family alive. It also provides the setting for creating memories utilizing all of the senses – sights, sounds, smells, tastes and touch. As the unofficial hub of family life, your kitchen deserves special blessing.

In this "heart of my home," may I shift my eyes from seeing endless work or clutter. Instead, may I be aware of the blessings represented in the constant flow of food, dishes, chatter and memories. As my loved ones mingle here, may we create not just delicious food, but also connections that nourish our spirits. May conversations flow easily as we work together. May we feel safe to tell our stories and express our joys, fears and dreams. May this room be filled with teamwork, generosity, gratitude, abundance, acceptance, humor and joy. May we live well in this sacred space.

Kitchen/Dining Table – Whether you have a separate dining room or not, the table where your family eats is a special spot in your home. Think of all the things that happen around a table! The stories from work or school, joking around, serious conversations, supervising homework, decorating Christmas cookies together, entertaining guests. If only your table could talk! Make sure you bless it often. (Note: if your family does not eat together, consider beginning to share 1-2 meals a week around the table. The benefits are tremendous and will help to create a more connected sense of family and home)

I give thanks for the precious moments shared around this table. May everyone who gathers around this table feel a sense of belonging whether they are here for an evening or a lifetime. May the food we share remind us that our needs are known and met. May the conversations held here be heartfelt, thought-provoking, uplifting and fun. As we share meals, tackle homework, decorate cookies, make crafts, discuss world events, plan vacations or even argue over differing opinions, may this table be a place of sincerity, connection and acceptance. May our hearts forever return to this place with fondness and the security of knowing that we are deeply loved.

Living/Family Room – Our family or "living" room is the space in our homes specifically designed for living. Here, we watch our favorite shows, play games, tussle on the floor with the kids, read books and entertain friends. Ironically, these rooms can also be a common spot for arguing, complaining and feeling lonely. (Ever watched a show alone and felt a deep inner ache?) Whether you live alone or in a family, bless this space often for it provides an important setting for your life.

In this room specifically set aside for living and gathering, may our hearts truly connect with one another. May our words and actions be laced with wisdom, compassion, humor and joy. May each person who shares this space feel included and valued. May happy, noisy moments fill us with energy and zest for life. May quiet, restorative moments heal and renew our spirits. In this room, may we send down deep family roots that provide shelter and strength for decades to come.

If you live alone, use this blessing:

In this room designed for living, may I create a beautiful life. May I use my time here wisely – not killing time or mindlessly "chilling," but may I balance relaxing with connection. In this room, may I hold great conversations with friends and family. May I engage in activities that feed my spirit and enrich my mind. May I pursue my dreams and passions with a joy that can only be called LIVING. May I feel at home in my home and may all loneliness or sadness be redirected into self-care and giving generously of my time and energy to loving others.

Bathroom – From cleansing and caring for our bodies, to bathing our children to clearing physical waste from our bodies, we spend a lot of important time in this room! Bathrooms also hold a deep emotional significance. We may have a love/hate relationship with the scale, the mirror or the nakedness of our body. In this room, we spend alone with ourselves, our thoughts and our bodies. Often, we make judgments about extra pounds, sagging skin or new wrinkles that deeply impact our lives. We definitely need to bless this space!!

As I gaze upon my reflection in the mirror, may my vision be guided by compassion, acceptance, tenderness and nurture. As I bathe my physical body, may I care for myself with kindness, washing away the stress and negativity of the day. May this room be a relaxing haven where my physical and emotional health improves daily. As I clear physical waste from my body, may all toxic emotional waste also be released. May I replace all self-judgment or criticism with consciously chosen thoughts that release and support abundant well-being. Within the privacy of this room, may I feel cherished and refreshed by my own love.

Child's Bedroom – A child's bedroom represents their personal world within the family home. Here they express creativity, play alone or with others, do homework, practice an instrument, daydream and rest their body and spirit. When a child feels afraid or sick, they usually retreat to their bedroom to seek comfort and nurture. Even a small child needs a haven from stress at school or even in the home.

Sadly, sometimes a child does not feel safe or at home in their room. Perhaps they feel tormented or frustrated by a sibling. Some children hide in their room to avoid hearing their parents argue. Others have experienced the violation of abuse in what should have been their safe space. In each of these situations, a child will need great patience and healing to regain a sense of safety and sanctuary.

During the teenage years, the child who once followed you everywhere suddenly withdraws – usually to their room. The closed bedroom door represents an important separation from the family. Your child is figuring out who he/she is apart from you and while challenging, this process is vital to their becoming a healthy individual. However, stay close. Behind their closed door, many teens battle loneliness, depression, heartbreak and many other strong emotions brought on by hormonal and physical stress. They may be holding you at arm's length, but they need your support more than ever.

Because the bedroom is so important in your child's life, it should be blessed regularly with special love – taking into consideration your child's specific needs. You can certainly include your child in the practice of blessing his/her room. However, I often blessed my children's rooms when they were not at home. Sitting on the bed, touching the pillow where they rest, perhaps holding a favorite piece of their clothing. I believe that blessing a child's room leaves behind the sacred fragrance of comfort, acceptance and love.

May this room be a haven of rest and renewal for _____.

As he/she spends time here, may he/she feel safe, sheltered, strengthened and cherished. May _____ be blessed with comfort when sad or lonely, peace when angry or worried, confidence when facing struggles or conflict, curiosity when playing or learning. May he/she enjoy meaningful connections with siblings or friends. May _____ sleep peacefully and be protected from frightening or unsettling dreams. Even at this young age, may he/she be divinely led in thought and action toward a purposeful and happy life.

Adult Bedroom – Within the walls of your bedroom, you open your eyes to day's first light and settle your mind and body for rest at the end of each day. Here you watch movies, read books, make love, cuddle your babies, have late-night pillow talk and sometimes (hopefully not too often) lie awake while your mind churns with plans, dreams or worries. If you don't have a partner or your relationship is struggling, your bedroom may also be a place of loneliness, longing or even bitterness. Beginning and ending each day with conscious Blessing is a powerful practice to activate the vibration you desire for this important room.

In this room, may I truly find sanctuary. May the toil, stress and worry of the day be released as I lie down and surrender my body to rest. May any conversations held in this space be loving. May I be freed from self-consciousness and self-protection so that I can give and receive true intimacy through words and touch. May loneliness drift away as I recall and rejoice in the heart connections I share with so many wonderful people. May my dreams be protected from evil or fear. May my body and spirit be restored each night so that I greet each new dawn with energy and joy.

Office – Your office may be a separate room, a desk in your bedroom or the corner of the kitchen table. Wherever you work, important decisions are made in this space as you pay bills, organize schedules, make phone calls and sign umpteen school papers. You may also run a home business from this space. If you struggle financially, this area of your home can be filled with tension, worry, frustration and "lack." Let's bless it!

I bless my office with order and peace. Each time I work here, may my mind be calm and my decisions made with clarity and wisdom. As I work to create a good life, may I see all finances as a river of blessing and generosity, flowing in and flowing out. May I have the courage to make necessary changes in my personal choices, finances and schedule in order to move closer to my dreams. May my eyes be opened to see the abundance of time, energy, resources and love that is mine.

Furnishings/Appliances/Tools – Imagine how difficult your life would be without running water, a couch, refrigerator, washer/dryer or lawnmower. Our furnishings and appliances bless our lives every day and we should return that blessing with gratitude. Because everything in our universe is composed of vibrating energy, even your appliances are affected by the atmosphere in your home. Have you ever noticed that when you're having a bad day, everything goes wrong? The toaster jams, the light bulb blows, the washer dies. An energy of chaos or frustration starts a chain reaction that affects even seemingly "inanimate" objects. When an item does wear out or break, thank it for its service. When you receive a new appliance or furnishing, welcome it as a team-member. Together, you are creating a home.

I give thanks for every labor-saving device in my home. May every appliance, tool and piece of furniture be blessed. (Feel free to bless them individually as you use them) May they operate efficiently and productively. May each item in my home be treated with kindness and respect by all who use them. May I always recognize and appreciate every part of my home and the privilege I have of owning and caring for these important items.

Other Rooms – Other rooms such as laundry rooms, pantries, storage spaces, basements or attics should also be blessed. Look around each space and ask yourself what purpose it fills in your home.

Perhaps you'll see things that need to be changed, reorganized or even discarded in order to free the space for greater purpose. You can write out your own blessing or just walk through the room, touching the walls and speaking the blessings that come to your mind. (Look at the "Catalog of Blessings" at the end of the book for ideas)

Yard/Porch/Patio – Outdoor spaces represent connection and fun as we grill delicious foods, play backyard games, host friends, grow vegetables, build a snow man or relax with an evening glass of wine. Yards can also be a learning space for cooperation and work ethic as our children help with mowing the lawn, shoveling snow, etc. Unspoken blessings such as lovely flower beds, colorful flags or a string of glowing lanterns can fill your outdoor atmosphere with a sense of beauty, relaxation, connection and an overall celebration of life. Even if you live in an apartment complex, you probably have a small entryway or at least a front door where you can intentionally create a beautiful welcome. Walk around your yard and bless it often!

I give thanks for my part of the earth – no matter how small. May I feel supported by the firmness of the earth beneath my feet. May my body and spirit be renewed by the beauty of trees, grass and flowers. May the sun and wind on my skin remind me that I am alive and intimately connected to this amazing world. May this yard/porch/patio be a place of connection and relaxation. May my loved ones and I work together in a spirit of fun and cooperation. May we play together with exuberance, delight and respect. May we relax together and be re-energized. May each person who spends time in this outdoor space feel loved and at home.

Vehicles – We spend a lot of time in our vehicles. From work commutes, school carpools, important appointments, long-awaited vacations, routine grocery shopping, school events and sports meets to visiting grandma, our vehicles transport us through many significant moments of our lives. Some of our most important conversations take place while the miles speed by. Work vehicles or trucks also play a vital role in providing for our family. Whether your car is new or used, it's a good idea to cleanse and bless it. Much like an appliance, it is a useful tool that can be affected by the emotions, energy and attitudes of past and present owners.

My life has been enriched greatly by the connections and opportunities made possible by this vehicle. As I have been blessed, I bless this vehicle with the respect and appreciation it deserves. May it operate with efficiency, ease and safety. May the hours spent in it be enjoyable. Together may we find adventure, experience the beauty of this world and nurture connection through fun and meaningful conversations with fellow travelers. When used for work, may this vehicle be blessed as it contributes to the provision and quality of my life. May I extend kindness and grace to other drivers and always operate this vehicle in a responsible and caring manner. May this car/truck be used to advance my story, my life purpose and the greater good of this world.

Home Blessing Ceremony

Planning

As with any event, a successful home Blessing Ceremony requires some basic planning. The first step is to determine the PURPOSE for holding a ceremony. There can be several reasons to hold a special event to bless your home.

- moving into a new home or apartment
- beginning a new chapter of life (new job, new relationship .. anything that represents a fresh start is a good time to cleanse the old and welcome the new)
- you feel the need to refresh the atmosphere after a particularly difficult time – an illness, a tragedy or a bout of depression.
- completing major renovation, spring cleaning or decluttering
- calendar events such as the new year or the beginning of a season (spring, summer, fall, etc)

Once you've decided the purpose for your Blessing Ceremony, you need to decide the Who, What and When basics of any celebration:

- Decide Who Will Attend - While a home blessing can be done alone, including your partner will add the power of agreement to your blessing. If you want to hold a religious blessing, you may wish to invite your pastor or priest. Other people invite close friends and family. You can make this an intimate occasion or a full-on party. It's up to you!
- Set the Date and Time - Schedule your home blessing for a time when the house will be quiet. If you have children, they will benefit greatly by participating. However, if you

have a very young child who may cry or be restless, you may
want to arrange for a stand-by babysitter or schedule the
ceremony after they're asleep.

- If possible, schedule the Blessing Ceremony for a nice day
when you can open windows and doors. You may also want
to walk around your yard as part of the ceremony. If you're
inviting others, create an invitation with the date, time and
location.

- Focus on Specific Blessings - Choose 2-3 specific blessings
that you want to be the focus for your home. What does your
heart need most? Joy? Hope? Courage? (Use the Catalog of
Blessings to help you think of options)

Gathering Supplies

Once you've set the time and date, you can focus on choosing
the spoken and unspoken blessings that will bless your home. You
can use a combination of spoken and unspoken blessings. This is
YOUR ceremony, so it can be completely customized to your time
and energy. Let's look at some ways you can invite your chosen
blessings.

Spoken Blessings – select a favorite poem, scripture or quote
that represents each blessing. You can also write your own blessings
for your home – perhaps a short blessing for each room. Write your
chosen blessings on individual cards so that they can be read by
yourself or others during the blessing ceremony.

Unspoken Blessings – Consider each of the five senses and
how you can add more emphasis to the mental act of blessing your
home. When you want to write a new chapter in your home's history,
remember that new synapses are formed immediately through
emotion. Creating a complete sensory experience for yourself and
your loved ones will make the power of Home Blessing even greater.

- Sight – choose a special piece of artwork, photo or figurine to symbolize each blessing you wish to invite. You could plant a rose bush or small tree to commemorate the occasion. If you have children, this would be a perfect time to imprint their hands in concrete. Purchase a blank canvas and have each person write a blessing on it. You can then frame this and hang it in your home.
- Sound – select a meaningful song to play during the ceremony. You can also hang a new wind chime or some other symbol that will remind you of this special day every time you hear its sound
- Smell – candles are often used in dedication or blessing ceremonies. You may want to give each participant their own candle or select one larger candle that is carried from room to room. Anointing oil also holds powerful symbolism for protection and blessing. You can order special oils online, use an essential oil that represents one of the blessings you desire or raid your kitchen for plain old olive or canola oil. The oil isn't as important as the intention you will use when you anoint your home. The oil becomes a symbol or carrier of the blessing you wish to infuse into the home.
- Taste – FOOD is an amazing way of blessing any event! Prepare your favorite dish or dessert or invite your guests to each bring something to share. If you're blessing your home alone, treat yourself to something special like a glass of wine or special chocolates.
- Touch – At some point during the ceremony, holding hands with your loved ones can symbolize unity and connection. You could also buy each person a new pair of pajamas or a blanket to help remember the event.

Before Your Guests Arrive

If possible, use some of the strategies in the Cleansing section to clear both the physical and spiritual space. Simple cleaning and decluttering will allow your home to start "fresh" as you begin a new chapter or season of life.

However, a clean house is NOT the point! Do not get hung up on this and postpone blessing your home because it isn't as clean as you'd like. No one is coming to critique your dust bunnies or baseboards. If you struggle with keeping your home clean, you may find that the act of blessing gives you greater energy and hope to tackle the clutter and chaos. Your home doesn't need to be spotless to be a blessed home!

Gather your supplies: the index cards with blessings written on them, any objects or items that represent the blessings, anointing oil, candles, food, or any other items that you've chosen as part of the day.

As you prepare for your guests to arrive, set an atmosphere of Blessing using soft music, a few lit candles and perhaps a fresh vase of flowers. Turn off your cellphones and eliminate as many distractions as possible. If the weather is nice, open windows and doors to air out your home.

The Ceremony
Adapt as needed to fit your situation or
your spiritual/religious beliefs.

1 - Begin on the lawn near the front door of your home. If the weather is not good, you can begin inside the home near the front door.

2 - Invite your guests to stand in a circle. Welcome them and thank them for being part of this special occasion in your home.

3 - Begin the ceremony by anointing the top of the front door frame while making a simple affirmation that you recognize and accept your role as the caretaker and guardian of your home's sacred space. You can use the "Claiming the Keys" statement from chapter one or use your own words.

4 - If you are outside, enter the home now. Ask each person to

silently agree with you while you speak the following declaration of dedication and protection for the home.

"As the spiritual caretaker of this space, I (we) give thanks for the blessing of this home. I (we) dedicate this home as a sanctuary of safety and security. Through my(our) God-given authority, I (we) cleanse this home from any past or present negativity, energy, emotions or actions and invite protecting angels to stand guard around this home so that no evil may enter. I (we) bless all the contents of the home, the property and vehicles. I (we) bless all who live here and those who visit. May all who enter this door find a welcome reprieve from the cares of the world. May each one be blessed with abundance and strength in mind, body, spirit, relationships, work or school and finances. When they leave this home, may they feel refreshed and blessed."

5 - Moving from room to room, anoint each doorway and window frame. Pause in each room and speak the blessings you've chosen. "I bless this room with _____, _____ and _____." If you have a special poem or verse that you've chosen for that room, have someone read it now. If you're using a candle, carry it with you from room to room, allowing its light to shine into each area of your home.

6 - If you've chosen a symbol or piece of artwork for a room, take a moment to place it in each room. Take time to explain its meaning. This is especially helpful for young children to understand what's happening. When they see that photo or object, they will remember this moment.

7 – Return to your living/family room. If you've carried a candle throughout your home, pass it around the circle now. Ask each person to speak a blessing for your home. If you're blessing your home alone, light the candle and spend a moment reflecting on the light that symbolizes warmth, cheer and the absence of darkness. Place the candle on your kitchen or dining room table and allow it to burn for an hour or so as a reminder of the blessings you've invited into your home.

8 – If you've invited a pastor or priest, they can now speak a prayer or blessing. They may incorporate specific prayers or rituals

that are essential to your faith. You can still design the rest of the ceremony to fit your personality and your family's needs. This would be a good time to hold hands with your loved ones to symbolize unity and togetherness in the blessing.

9 - If you own your own property, you can include walking the boundaries of your land as part of your Blessing Ceremony. As you walk, speak out the blessings you desire. You can also use the "Walking the Land" blessing. If you don't feel comfortable speaking aloud (perhaps you have close neighbors), you can walk silently while praying or focusing on the intention of the blessings you desire.

10 - Conclude the ceremony by sharing a simple treat or meal with your partner or guests. If you're blessing your home alone, be sure not to skip this part. Nourishing yourself with a special treat will send a powerful message to your body and spirit.

If you have enough time, you can plan a brief activity to celebrate and bless the purpose of each room. Here are some examples:

- living/family room - play a short game
- bedroom - have each person close their eyes and be still for a moment to represent rest
- child's bedroom - have each person speak a blessing to the child
- bathroom - have each person wash their hands with special soap
- kitchen – prepare a simple snack together (mini-pizzas with toppings, ice cream sundaes)
- dining room - gather around the table to share the snack.

Remember that there is no right or wrong way to bless your home. Any blessing is a blessing!

Thank You

My heart is filled with gratitude for the amazing people who have contributed to this book – many without realizing it! While I cannot recognize or thank them all, I want to honor a few who have shaped my journey as a spirit having a human experience:

- My birthmother – you gave me life and your body was my first earthly home
- Mrs. Keefer – your foster home sheltered me during the first months of my life as you became my first nurturer
- Mom and Dad – you gave me the gift of a forever family and modeled the beauty of a simple, but well-lived life
- Heidi – every time I took the experts' advice to "write to one person," you were my person. As one of my earliest readers, your honest input from "life's trenches" has been invaluable!
- Karen, Erin, Robin, Karianne, Martha, Wes and Aunt Phyllis – as my faithful cheerleaders, you've given me the courage to return to the page month after month
- Christian, Katie, Sodie, CorrieAnne and Tyrell – without you, my home would have been quiet and boring! You have made me laugh, cry, scream, learn, grow and love in ways I could not have imagined. You're my motivation to be the best human being possible!
- Wayne – no one else understands this crazy journey like you do. Every step has required courage, patience and a solid sense of humor. Together, we have created a home.

May the Lord bless you
and keep you

May the Lord make his
face to shine upon you
and be gracious to you

May the Lord lift up his
countenance upon you
and give you peace

CHRISTIAN BLESSING

Resources

RESOURCES

End Notes

1   Jeremiah 1:5, New International Version
2   Glennon Doyle, *Love Warrior,* New York: Flatiron Books, 2016
3   Bruce Lipton, *The Biology of Belief 10th Anniversary Edition*, Hay House, 2016
4   Stephen Sinatra, *What is Earthing or Grounding,* HeartMD Institute, 2018
5   Marla Cilley, *Sink Reflections,* Bantam Books, 2002
6   Ephesians 4:26, New International Version
7   Hebrews 12:1, New International Version
8   Matthew 18:20, New International Version
9   https://thrivinglaunch.com/the-power-of-belief-bruce-lipton/
10   https://www.ikeahackers.net/2018/05/ikea-bully-a-plant-experiment.html
11   Genesis 1:1-3, New International Version
12   Proverbs 15:4, New Living Translation
13   Proverbs 18:4, Berean Study Bible
14   Loretta Graciano Bruening, *Habits of a Happy Brain*, Adams Media, 2015
15   Matthew 12:34, New International Version
16   Daniel Halpern, *How to Eat Alone,* https://www.haggardandhalloo.com/2010/10/23/eat/
17   https://www.challahconnection.com/jewish-housewarming/
18   Hal Elrod, *The Miracle Morning: The 6 Habits That Will Transform Your Life Before 8AM,* John Murray Learning, 2017

Resources for Releasing/ Clearing Emotions

Bradley Nelson, *The Emotion Code: How to Release Your Trapped Emotions for Abundant Health, Love and Happiness*, New York: St Martin's Essentials, 2019

Emotional Freedom Technique, www.emofree.com

Nick Ortner, *The Tapping Solution: A Revolutionary System for Stress Free Living*, Hay   House, 2014

Resources for Caring for Your Physical Home

Routines and support for eliminating clutter, organizing and menu planning - www.flylady.net

Meal Planning - https://www.thekitchn.com/the-beginners-guide-to-meal-planning-what-to-know-how-to-succeed-and-what-to-skip-242413

Essential Oil Suppliers -
DoTerra – www.doterra.com
Young Living – www.youngliving.com

(It is important to buy pure essential oils. These two companies are very reputable and uphold high standards for harvesting and distilling their oils. For both companies, you will need to purchase through a distributor. You can find a distributor through these websites or you may already know a family member or friend who sells these essential oils.)

Catalog of Blessings

abundance
acceptance
adventure
affection
aliveness
amusement
anticipation
appreciation
awareness
awe
balance
beauty
belonging
calmness
cheerfulness
cherished (feeling of being)
clarity
comfort
commitment
companionship
compass
confidence
connection
contentment
conversation
cooperation
courage
creativity
curiosity

delight
diligence
efficiency
empathy
encouragement
energy
excitement
faith
focus
forgiveness
freedom
friendship
fulfillment
fun
generosity
gentleness
gratitude
happiness
harmony
helpfulness
honor
hope
humor
imagination
inspiration
intimacy
joy
kindness
laughter

listening
love
loyalty
maturity
mercy
motivation
nurture
openness
passion
patience
peace
playfulness
pleasure
pride
productivity
purpose
radiance
refreshment
relaxation
relief
resourcefulness
responsibility
rest
restoration
safety
satisfaction
security
self-care
serenity
simplicity
sincerity
strength
teamwork
tenderness

thoughtfulness
togetherness
trust
understanding
vision
well-being
wisdom
wonder
youthfulness